The Bride's Book of Lists

Things to Do & Questions to Ask

Amy Nebens

Illustrations by Greg Stadler

STERLING

New York / London
www.sterlingpublishing.com

STERLING and the distinctive Sterling logo are registered trademarks of
Sterling Publishing Co., Inc.

Library of Congress Cataloging-in-Publication Data Available

16   18   20   19   17

Published by Sterling Publishing Co., Inc.
387 Park Avenue South, New York, NY 10016
© 2003 by Barnes & Noble Publishing, Inc.
Distributed in Canada by Sterling Publishing
c/o Canadian Manda Group, 165 Dufferin Street
Toronto, Ontario, Canada M6K 3H6
Distributed in the United Kingdom by GMC Distribution Services
Castle Place, 166 High Street, Lewes, East Sussex, England BN7 1XU
Distributed in Australia by Capricorn Link (Australia) Pty. Ltd.
P.O. Box 704, Windsor, NSW 2756, Australia

Illustrations: © Greg Stadler

Sterling ISBN-13: 978-0-7607-4231-0
ISBN-10: 0-7607-4231-6

For information about custom editions, special sales, premium and
corporate purchases, please contact Sterling Special Sales
Department at 800-805-5489 or specialsales@sterlingpublishing.com.

Contents

Introduction

He proposed and you accepted—or maybe it was the other way around. Either way, the result is wonderfully the same. You are engaged—and about to embark upon an amazing journey together. Along the way, you will encounter endless well wishes, delightful stacks of presents, and perhaps even a celebration or two in your honor. Enjoy this time; there is nothing else like it.

That said, there is also much work to be done. After all, you have a wedding to plan—an endeavor that is both exciting and challenging. But all the time and energy devoted to organizing this momentous occasion will seem worth it on the big day when you stand before family and friends to be pronounced husband and wife.

The purpose of this book is to facilitate your planning efforts by providing you with the information you need and the right questions to ask—in a streamlined, efficient format. To make navigating easier, topics are organized into ten sections, clearly marked with tabs. Within each section, you'll find detailed lists of "things to do," helpful tips and advice, and prepared interviews for meeting with service providers—complete with questions to pose before hiring and spaces to record responses. There is also space at the end of each interview, as well as at the end of each section, for you to write additional notes. In an attempt to be comprehensive, we've included a wide range of topics and questions; of course, not all brides will have the same concerns and desires, so make use of only those elements that apply to your situation.

Before turning to any one section, take the time to look through the introduction. Here, you'll find such helpful tools as a planning timeline, a budget worksheet, a list of valuable money-saving tips, and guidelines to follow when hiring wedding professionals. The appendix at the back of the book offers additional planning aids, which are listed in the table of contents.

The folders located on the inside front and back covers are a convenient place to store magazine clippings and any leaflets you may receive from service providers; for added convenience, you can stash business cards in the translucent plastic sleeves at the front of the book. As a record of your meetings, this book will not only help you stay organized, it will prove useful to have on hand during subsequent meetings for reference purposes and to allow you to make quick comparisons on the spot. And when the planning is over and the party has begun, just tuck your book away until a time, years from now, when you want to remember the details of how your wedding day came to be.

Planning Timeline

Here, you'll find a general overview of the steps involved in the planning process. Once you get an idea of what's ahead, refer to the "things to do" checklists within each section for detailed accounts. Keep in mind that it's never too early to start planning. Locations, bands, photographers, even officiants can be booked up more than a year in advance. While the planner below can be used as a guide for budgeting your time, the earlier you make arrangements, the better. And, of course, use common sense—if certain elements of the wedding are more important to you than others, you may want to focus on them first. The schedule below begins nine months before the wedding, but that's not to say that you'll have to settle for less if you've got less time—just get started now.

NINE MONTHS BEFORE OR EARLIER

- ☐ Plan get-together for families to meet, celebrate, and discuss wedding plans
- ☐ Announce engagement in newspapers
- ☐ Discuss budget—with each other and family (include both families in talks if both families will be sharing the costs)
- ☐ Select a date—and alternative ones so you can be flexible when it comes to the availability of a location or a wedding professional you want to hire
- ☐ Go for engagement photograph sitting
- ☐ Hire wedding consultant (see page 50 to determine whether or not you want to enlist the help of such a professional)
- ☐ Choose and ask attendants
- ☐ Put together guest list
- ☐ Book site for ceremony
- ☐ Book site for reception
- ☐ Book officiant
- ☐ Book caterer
- ☐ Book musicians for ceremony
- ☐ Book band/disc jockey for reception
- ☐ Order dress and veil/headpiece

SIX TO NINE MONTHS BEFORE

- ☐ Book photographer
- ☐ Book videographer
- ☐ Book florist
- ☐ Select and order attendants' dresses and accessories
- ☐ Reserve rental equipment, including tent, tables, chairs, linens, china, and any other necessities
- ☐ Meet with caterer to plan menu and schedule tasting
- ☐ Order invitations and other wedding stationery
- ☐ Book calligrapher
- ☐ Send save-the-date cards to out-of-town guests
- ☐ If having an at-home wedding, begin any necessary home improvements and/or landscaping work
- ☐ Make arrangements with hotel to hold block of rooms for out-of-town guests
- ☐ Book room for your wedding night
- ☐ Investigate honeymoon destinations and travel arrangements

- If traveling abroad, update passports, visas, and any other required travel documents and inquire about necessary immunizations
- Register for wedding gifts

FOUR TO SIX MONTHS BEFORE
- Make final honeymoon reservations
- Purchase/order/make favors
- Schedule time for ceremony rehearsal
- Plan rehearsal dinner (whether this involves making the arrangements yourself or discussing the event with the groom's family)
- Purchase tuxedo/suit, or reserve rental (groom and groomsmen)
- Meet with florist to discuss and decide upon bouquets, arrangements, etc.
- Order wedding cake
- Purchase/order/make gifts for bridal party
- Purchase bridal shoes and other accessories
- Have invitations addressed

TWO TO FOUR MONTHS BEFORE
- Send hotel, transportation, and area attractions information to out-of-town guests (if wedding is in a popular tourist destination during peak season, you may want to do this earlier)
- Investigate local requirements for obtaining marriage license
- Book/arrange for transportation for bride, groom, attendants, and immediate family on wedding day

- Meet with officiant to discuss service
- If writing your own vows, begin doing so now
- Select readings/songs for ceremony; ask those you want to read/perform if they will do the honor
- Make selections for ceremony music
- Select songs for the major highlights of reception (first dance, cake-cutting, bouquet toss, etc.)
- Purchase appropriate undergarments and hosiery for wedding gown, and bring to first fitting
- Purchase wedding rings
- Select gift for groom, if you two are exchanging presents
- Select thank-you gifts for parents
- Purchase going-away outfit
- Mail invitations (this should be done six to eight weeks before wedding)
- Investigate local newspapers' time requirements and content guidelines for wedding announcements
- Have wedding portrait taken
- Do trial runs with makeup artist and hairstylist, and schedule beauty appointments for the wedding day

FOUR TO SIX WEEKS BEFORE
- Make arrangements for blood tests, if state requires (check with the local town clerk's office to find out if and when exactly this needs to be done)
- Obtain marriage license (the time period during which this needs to be done varies according to local regulations; check with the local town clerk's office)

- [ ] Create/order ceremony programs
- [ ] Plan bridesmaids' luncheon
- [ ] Put together welcome baskets for out-of-town guests
- [ ] Send wedding announcements to newspapers
- [ ] Give list of songs you want (and don't want) played to band/disc jockey
- [ ] Have final dress fitting
- [ ] Pick up ordered tuxedo/suit, if purchasing (groom and groomsmen)
- [ ] Start arranging seating plan
- [ ] Pick up wedding rings

TWO WEEKS BEFORE

- [ ] Give caterer final head count
- [ ] Finalize seating plan; write place cards, or give calligrapher the information and materials to do so
- [ ] Send shot lists to photographer and videographer
- [ ] Compose toasts for rehearsal dinner and wedding reception
- [ ] Make a detailed schedule of the wedding reception events (times for cocktails, first dance, dinner, cake-cutting, etc.) to give to all applicable service providers
- [ ] Break in shoes and scuff bottoms

ONE WEEK BEFORE

- [ ] Pick up dress, if not being delivered
- [ ] Pick up tuxedo, if renting (groom and groomsmen)
- [ ] Confirm reservations for wedding night and honeymoon

- [ ] Get crisp bills from bank for gratuities; put tips in labeled envelopes and seal
- [ ] Organize final payments for service providers who need to be paid on wedding day
- [ ] Pack for honeymoon
- [ ] Purchase traveler's checks
- [ ] Make a list of everything you need to bring to wedding, and gather all the necessary items together
- [ ] Host bridesmaids' luncheon (often done the day before the wedding to accommodate out-of-town attendants)
- [ ] Confirm final details with all service providers
- [ ] Have mail held at post office
- [ ] Call stores where you're registered to hold deliveries

ONE DAY BEFORE

- [ ] Drop off welcome baskets for out-of-town guests at hotel (or ask attendant to do so)
- [ ] Get manicure and pedicure
- [ ] Have rehearsal; hand out gifts to wedding party if you haven't already done so
- [ ] Assign tasks and duties to wedding party for next day
- [ ] Give attendants anything they need to execute said duties
- [ ] Attend rehearsal dinner
- [ ] Give groom his gift, if you two are exchanging presents

Budget Planner

Knowing just how much you are able to spend will facilitate the planning process and help you to make decisions. Be sure to account for taxes and gratuities, which often are not included in quoted fees. For a typical wedding, you can expect to devote roughly the following percentages of your budget toward specified aspects: 50% for reception; 10% for music; 10% for flowers; 10% for photography/videography; 10% for bride's and groom's attire; 10% for the remaining expenses (invitations, transportation, etc.). Use the worksheet below to help outline your costs.

Wedding Element	Estimate	Actual	Deposit	Balance
RECEPTION (50%)				
Site fee				
Food/caterer				
Bar/corkage fee				
Champagne/wine				
Cake/cake-cutting fee				
Rentals				
Wedding consultant				
Parking fees/valet parking				
Coat check attendant				
Gratuities				
Subtotal				
MUSIC (10%)				
Ceremony musicians				
Music for cocktail hour				
Band/disc jockey for reception				
Subtotal				
FLOWERS/DECORATIONS (10%)				
Ceremony site flowers/decorations				
Bride's bouquet				
Maid of honor's bouquet				
Bridesmaids' bouquets				
Toss bouquet				
Corsages				
Boutonnieres				
Flower girls' baskets				
Floral hair accessories				

Wedding Element	Estimate	Actual	Deposit	Balance
Reception centerpieces				
Arrangements for buffet tables				
Arrangements for cake table				
Arrangements for rest rooms				
Other reception decorations				
Subtotal				
PHOTOGRAPHY/VIDEOGRAPHY (10%)				
Photography package/fee				
Wedding album (if not included in above)				
Additional albums				
Additional prints				
Negatives				
Videography package/fee				
Additional videos				
Disposable cameras (for tables) and developing costs				
Subtotal				
ATTIRE/BEAUTY (10%)				
Bridal gown				
Alterations				
Veil/headpiece				
Shoes				
Undergarments				
Hosiery				
Jewelry				
Other accessories				
Rehearsal dinner outfit				
Going-away outfit				
Hair				
Makeup				
Manicure/pedicure				
Groom's tuxedo/suit				
Groom's shoes/socks				
Groom's accessories (bow tie/tie, cumberbund/vest, cuff links, studs, braces, etc.)				
Subtotal				

Wedding Element	Estimate	Actual	Deposit	Balance
OTHER EXPENSES (10%)				
CEREMONY				
Site fee				
Officiant's fee/donation				
Ceremonial objects/accessories (unity candle, wine goblet, etc.)				
Ring bearer's pillow				
Marriage license				
Wedding rings				
Subtotal				
STATIONERY				
Wedding invitations				
Save-the-date cards				
At-home cards				
Announcements				
Thank-you notes				
Ceremony programs				
Menus				
Seating cards				
Calligrapher's fee				
Postage (for invitations, response cards, thank-you notes, information packets for out-of-town guests, etc.)				
Other				
Subtotal				
TRANSPORTATION				
Rented vehicle(s) for bride, groom, immediate family, and wedding party				
Gratuities for drivers				
Shuttle for guests				
Subtotal				
GIFTS				
Favors				
Welcome baskets for out-of-town guests				
Gifts for wedding party				
Gifts for parents				
Bride and groom's gifts to each other				
Subtotal				

Wedding Element	Estimate	Actual	Deposit	Balance
PARTIES				
Bridesmaids' luncheon				
Rehearsal dinner				
Subtotal				
MISCELLANEOUS				
TOTAL				

Money-Saving Hints and Tips

✧ The going rate for location fees in January, February, and March is typically lower than at other times of the year.

✧ Some locations charge a higher fee for Saturday nights as opposed to other times in the week.

✧ Typically buffet-style meals are less pricey than seated ones, and cocktail receptions cost less than buffets; breakfasts, brunches, and afternoons are usually less costly still.

✧ Ask caterers about bringing in your own liquor. You may be able to save money if you buy it wholesale; just be sure to find out if the caterer charges a corkage fee (a fee for "opening" bottles you provide).

✧ Skip the "champagne toast," and let guests raise glasses of whatever they're drinking; doing so can shave off as much as $5 per person.

✧ If you need to rent chairs for both the ceremony and reception, try to get ones that work for both rather than renting two different sets. Make sure that doing this won't pose any setup problems.

✧ Make engagement announcements or rehearsal dinner invites yourself with store-bought stationery run through a home computer; doing so will leave more money to spend on professionally printed wedding invitations.

✧ Classic black ink is typically less expensive than colored ink.

✧ Classic white or ivory paper is typically less expensive than colored paper.

✧ Keep calligraphy costs down by enlisting the help of an artistic friend to address invitations or write out seating cards.

✧ Consider hiring a disc jockey instead of a band, as fees for the former are typically less expensive.

✧ Have the band or disc jockey stop playing at the appointed hour (just after the bride and groom have made their exit); this way you won't incur overtime charges for the music or the site (a band packing up is a sure sign to guests that the party is over).

✧ Avoid having a wedding around such holidays as Valentine's Day and Mother's Day, when flower prices are higher.

◇ Use seasonal flowers for bouquets and arrangements; they are less expensive than out-of-season blooms.

◇ Consider alternatives to traditional floral centerpieces, such as arrangements of greenery, bowls of fruit, or compotes artistically stacked with pretty wrapped favors.

◇ You may be able to get a discount if you hire a photographer and a videographer from the same studio.

◇ Wear your mother's wedding gown—for the sentiment as well as the savings.

◇ If purchasing favors, ask for a bulk discount or wholesale rate.

Hiring Guidelines

◇ When starting your search for locations and service providers, check with friends and family members for suggestions and referrals. Site coordinators and catering managers are also good resources for recommendations.

◇ Before scheduling an interview with a service provider, inquire as to whether he/she is available for your wedding date and time.

◇ Just because a professional is highly recommended by a friend or relative doesn't mean you don't have to interview him/her. You need to make sure that the service provider's way of thinking is in line with yours.

◇ During the interview process, make sure that you get the answers you are looking for and that you feel comfortable with the person. If not, move on.

◇ It's a good idea to meet with more than one service provider before making a hiring decision so you get a sense of your options. Keep the meetings limited, though; too many will just make your head swim.

◇ Ask for three references. If a professional doesn't agree to provide names and contact information, it's a sure sign to move on.

◇ Once you find the service providers you want, go ahead and book them—soon. Chances are, if you like them, they're good, and their schedules fill up quickly.

◇ Make sure that your contracts state: dates, times (arrival and departure), location of wedding, fees (including taxes and overtime charges; noting gratuities is optional), deposit amount, balance due date and amount, insurance coverage, cancellation and refund policies, names of the people who will provide the service, agreed-upon attire of professionals, number and length of breaks, meal accommodations, and detailed descriptions of absolutely everything that is being provided.

◇ If you're unsure of contract terms, you may want to have a lawyer review the documents.

◇ Don't work with any professional who expects payment in full before services are rendered. A partial deposit, however, is acceptable and, in most cases, expected.

Chapter One

Ceremony

Ceremony

Things to Do

- [ ] Make appointments to meet with site coordinators and/or officiants
- [ ] Visit potential ceremony sites
- [ ] Reserve location for date of wedding
- [ ] Send signed contract and deposit for ceremony site
- [ ] Choose and ask attendants
- [ ] Book officiant
- [ ] Reserve any necessary rental equipment (see page 56)
- [ ] Schedule rehearsal
- [ ] Schedule any necessary meetings/counseling sessions with officiant
- [ ] Make arrangements for ceremony music (see page 81)
- [ ] Make arrangements for floral decorations (see page 97)
- [ ] Make arrangements for any other decorations for ceremony site
- [ ] Consult local town clerk's office regarding marriage license requirements:
  - [ ] how far in advance you need to and are able to obtain license
  - [ ] what jurisdiction license needs to be from (where you'll be married or where you live)
  - [ ] witness requirements
  - [ ] whether a blood test is required and what must be tested for
  - [ ] where you can get the blood test
- [ ] Get blood tests, if required
- [ ] Obtain marriage license
- [ ] Obtain any necessary official religious documents
- [ ] Plan/write vows
- [ ] Plan/adapt/review any other parts of ceremony
- [ ] Select readings and/or songs for special participants
- [ ] Send selected readings and/or songs to appropriate participants
- [ ] Decide upon order of attendants for processional
- [ ] Make any desired seating arrangements
- [ ] Arrange for place to get dressed before ceremony
- [ ] Determine where to have receiving line (could be done at reception site instead)
- [ ] Obtain any objects necessary for ceremony customs, such as drinking wine from a shared goblet, lighting the unity candle, or breaking the glass
- [ ] Obtain pillow for ring bearer
- [ ] Purchase birdseed/bubbles for guests to shower you with as you leave ceremony site (this custom could instead be performed as you leave the reception site)

☐ Make arrangements for distribution of ceremony programs and/or signing of guest book

☐ Assign attendant to arrange dress and/or veil at altar

☐ Put together emergency supply kit for wedding day (see page 157 for contents)

☐ Arrange for someone to hold or a place to keep emergency kit during ceremony (and reception)

☐ Confirm final details/times with officiant and site coordinator

☐ Get contact numbers for officiant and site coordinator for wedding day

☐ Other _____

☐ _____

☐ _____

Site

Questions to Ask: Ceremony Site

Ceremony Site I

Site name:

Contact person:

Address:

Phone/Fax:

E-mail:

❤ What dates and times are available?

❤ How many people does the space hold—seated and standing?

❤ If the space is bigger than we need, can pews or rows be roped off?

❤ *If a house of worship:* Will any congregant or other worshiper be permitted to attend the ceremony?

❤ *If an outdoor location:* Is there a backup plan for inclement weather? An indoor alternative?

Words to the Wise

✧ If you're planning to hold your ceremony and reception in two different places, the distance that you and your guests will need to travel between the two should factor into your selection of sites.

✧ If you're considering having your ceremony in a public outdoor space (such as a beach or park), find out if you need to acquire a permit or any special permissions.

✧ Asking a dear friend to do a reading or requesting that a musically gifted relative sing a song at your wedding is a good way to personalize your ceremony while honoring someone close to you.

✧ For an outdoor ceremony on a hot day, consider having waiters circulate with glasses of water for guests.

Ceremony Site II	*Ceremony Site III*

Ceremony Site I

❤ What are the acoustics like?

❤ Will the officiant use/need
a microphone?

❤ Will we or any readers be heard
easily without a microphone?
Is one available if necessary?

❤ How long is the aisle?

❤ Is there a room in which my
attendants and I can dress?

❤ Is there an organ or piano?

❤ Can we hire an outside musician
to play it?

❤ Can other musicians be brought in
to play other instruments?

❤ Are there any restrictions regarding
instruments or music?

❤ Is there space for musicians to set up?

❤ Are there ample electrical outlets
to suit their needs?

❤ Is photography or videography
permitted in the room?

❤ Is there a good spot to take
formal pictures?

❤ Can we bring in our own flowers?

❤ *If a house of worship:* Do couples
typically donate ceremony flowers to
the house of worship, or can we use
them for the reception?

❤ Are other decorations permitted?

❤ Is there someone on staff to help
coordinate a rehearsal?

❤ Is there someone on staff to help
coordinate such details as seating
the guests, cuing members of the
processional, and setting up a table
for programs?

Ceremony Site II

Ceremony Site III

Ceremony Site I

💟 Is there a suitable spot for a
receiving line? _____

💟 Will any other ceremonies be
taking place at the same time? _____
On the same day? _____

💟 Is throwing birdseed or blowing
bubbles allowed after the ceremony? _____
Is there a place to do this? _____

💟 Is there parking? _____
If so, what is the capacity? _____

💟 Does the facility have liability
insurance? _____

💟 What is the fee for use of the site? _____

💟 How much of a deposit is required? _____

💟 When is the balance due? _____

💟 What is the cancellation policy? _____

_____

_____

💟 Other questions/notes: _____

_____ _____

_____ _____

_____ _____

_____ _____

_____ _____

_____ _____

KEEP IN MIND
For the receiving line, the bride and her attendants should either set
aside their bouquets or hold their flowers in the left hand in order to
shake with the right.

Ceremony Site II   *Ceremony Site III*

Officiant

Questions to Ask: Religious Ceremony

Officiant I

Name:

Address:

Phone/Fax:

E-mail:

❧ What dates and times are you available?

❧ Can you give us an overview of the service?

❧ What are your thoughts about the service?

❧ How long is the typical ceremony?

❧ Can we help personalize the ceremony? If so, will you provide guidelines?

❧ Can we write our own vows? If so, will you provide guidance?

❧ Can we include family members/ friends in the service by assigning readings/prayers or songs?

❧ *If interfaith marriage:* Can another officiant (of the other faith) take part in the service?

❧ Will you perform the ceremony outside a house of worship?

❧ If the wedding is out of town, will you travel?

❧ Will you give a sermon or speech? If so, can we see a copy of what you'll say before the wedding?

❧ Do you permit photography or videography during the ceremony?

Officiant II

Officiant III

Officiant I

❧ Do you have any restrictions
regarding music? _____
❧ Are there restrictions regarding _____
wedding attire? _____
_____
❧ Will you attend the rehearsal? _____
❧ What is expected of us in terms of _____
premarital classes? _____
❧ How many pre-wedding meetings _____
will we have with you? _____
❧ When and where will the marriage _____
license be signed? _____
❧ How many witnesses are needed to _____
sign the marriage license? _____
❧ Are there any requirements regarding _____
who can be a witness? _____
❧ Is there a fee, or is a donation _____
acceptable? _____
❧ Other questions/notes: _____

_____　_____
_____　_____
_____　_____
_____　_____
_____　_____

KEEP IN MIND
Be sure to include your officiant and his or her spouse on the wedding
guest list.

Officiant II   *Officiant III*

Questions to Ask: Civil Ceremony

Officiant I

Name:

Address:

Phone/Fax:

E-mail:

❦ What dates and times are you available?

❦ Can you give us an overview of the ceremony?

❦ How long is the typical ceremony?

❦ How much guidance can we expect in shaping the ceremony?

❦ Can we write our own vows? Do you provide any guidelines?

❦ Can you provide us with standard vows if we don't write our own?

❦ Can any religious elements (readings, music, etc.) be included?

❦ Will you give a sermon or speech? Can we see a copy ahead of time?

❦ In terms of location, what is the extent of your jurisdiction?

❦ Will you travel within the area of your jurisdiction?

❦ What is expected of us in terms of premarital meetings?

❦ Will you attend the rehearsal?

❦ When, where, and by whom will the marriage license be signed?

❦ What is your fee?

❦ Other questions/notes:

Officiant II	Officiant III

Notes

Chapter Two

Reception

Reception

Things to Do

- [ ] Make appointments with site managers and, if necessary, caterers
- [ ] Hire wedding consultant (optional; see page 50)
- [ ] Visit potential reception sites
- [ ] Reserve location for date of wedding
- [ ] Send signed contract and deposit for location
- [ ] Interview potential caterers (if off-site)
- [ ] Book caterer
- [ ] Send signed contract and deposit to caterer
- [ ] Schedule menu tasting
- [ ] Take care of necessary home improvements/landscaping, if having at-home wedding
- [ ] Make arrangements for reception music (see page 84)
- [ ] Make arrangements for floral decorations (see page 97)
- [ ] Make arrangements for other reception decorations
- [ ] Make menu selections (see page 39 for menu checklist)
- [ ] Visit rentals showroom to choose chairs, tables, linens, china, etc.
- [ ] Reserve rental equipment (see page 56 for rentals worksheet)
- [ ] Schedule delivery and pickup of rental equipment
- [ ] Schedule cake tasting
- [ ] Order wedding cake (and groom's cake, if desired)
- [ ] Select cake topper
- [ ] Make arrangements for parking, if necessary
- [ ] Arrange for place to change into going-away outfits
- [ ] Give caterer and/or site coordinator final head count
- [ ] Make seating chart
- [ ] Compose toasts (from you to your groom; from the two of you thanking your hosts and guests)
- [ ] Confirm details, date, times, and location with rental company
- [ ] Get phone number of rental company contact for wedding day
- [ ] Confirm details with caterer
- [ ] Get phone number of caterer for wedding day
- [ ] Go over times for all reception "events" (cocktails, first dance, dinner, cake-cutting, etc.) with caterer/site coordinator, and give this schedule to applicable service providers (photographer, videographer, band/disc jockey)
- [ ] Get phone number of site coordinator for wedding day
- [ ] Give site coordinator arrival times for all service providers

☐ Ask caterer/site coordinator to have cake topper packed up for you, if yours to keep

☐ Ask caterer/site coordinator to have top tier of wedding cake packed up for you (to save for first anniversary)

☐ Assign someone to take top tier of wedding cake home and freeze for you—and to take cake topper home if applicable

☐ Arrange to have groom's cake cut up and boxed for favors, if desired (legend has it that a single woman who sleeps with some of this cake under her pillow will dream of her husband-to-be)

☐ Other _____

☐ _____

☐ _____

☐ _____

☐ _____

☐ _____

☐ _____

KEEP IN MIND

Help make your guests comfortable during the reception by placing baskets filled with useful items—such as adhesive bandages, hair spray, and mouthwash—in the rest rooms.

Site

Things to think about when deciding upon a reception location:
✧ Does the style of the space match the desired mood for your wedding?
✧ Does the decor coordinate with your desired color scheme?
✧ What are the views like?
✧ Are you comfortable with the site coordinator? (If you will be dealing with this person a lot, this is an important point.)

Things to think about if considering an at-home wedding:
✧ Do you have enough space to accommodate the number of people on your guest list?
✧ Will you be holding the event indoors, outdoors, or both?
✧ If outdoors, what will your backup plan be for inclement weather? Tent? Move everyone indoors?
✧ Will you be comfortable having a potentially large group of people in your home? (Remember there's always the possibility of breakage and spills.)
✧ Will you need to make any home improvements or do any landscaping before the event?
✧ How much rearranging of furniture will you need to do to accommodate the event?
✧ What items will you need to rent, and how much of an expense will this add?
✧ Will you be having the event catered, or will a family member be doing the cooking?
✧ Is there enough cooking space in your kitchen, or will you need to make other arrangements?
✧ Do you have enough parking space, and how will parking be organized?
✧ Do you have enough bathrooms, or will you need to rent portable toilets?

Things to think about if considering an outdoor wedding:
✧ What will your backup plan be in case of rain?
✧ Are you willing to risk having guests be uncomfortable due to extreme temperatures or excessive wind, or will you rent a tent equipped to temper the effects of such problems?
✧ Is the ground even enough for chairs and tables to be stable?
✧ What will the landscape (flowers and trees) look like at the time of the wedding? (Ask to see photographs.)
✧ Will allergies to outdoor elements affect your or the groom's enjoyment of the day?
✧ How will you combat insects that might be milling around after dark?
✧ If a public space, is a permit required?

Questions to Ask: Reception Site

For places with on-site caterers, the site coordinator may be the person with whom you will speak regarding the menu; if this is the case for your situation, refer to the list of catering questions that begins on page 38 during your interview.

Reception Site I

Site name:

Contact person:

Address:

Phone/Fax:

E-mail:

❧ What dates and times are available?

❧ What is the fee for the site rental?

❧ How many hours does that include?

❧ How much of that time is party time
and how much is setup and cleanup?

❧ How do overtime charges work?

❧ How many people can the space
comfortably accommodate for
a seated dinner?

❧ How many people can the space hold
for a cocktail reception (standing room
with some tables sprinkled about)?

❧ Are there any circumstances that
affect the capacity of the space
(for instance, the addition of a
dance floor or head table)?

❧ Do you provide tables, chairs, linens,
china, and glassware?

❧ Is there a choice of styles for any of
the above?

❧ *If tables are provided:* How many
guests per table?

Reception Site II · *Reception Site III*

Reception Site 1

- Can tables and chairs easily be placed in the reception area?
- How does the flow work if more than one room/area is used?
- *If using site for ceremony and reception:* Where will each take place?
- *If ceremony and reception are in the same room:* How will the space be transformed? How long will the changeover take?
- Where will cocktails be served?
- *If outdoors:* Is the ground even enough to set out chairs and tables for a cocktail hour and/or the reception?
- *If outdoors:* Is this a public space where anybody can wander in and out?
- *If outdoors:* Is there a backup plan for inclement weather?
- Are other spaces (gardens, terraces) accessible to guests?
- Are there additional charges for the use of other spaces?
- Are any spaces off-limits to guests?
- Will other parties be going on at the same time?
- Is there a party immediately preceding or following our event?
- If so, what preparations are taken to ensure that each party finishes on time, but no one is rushed out?
- *If a summer wedding:* Is the space air-conditioned?
- Is there an on-site coordinator?
- Will he/she or someone else be there on the wedding day to accept deliveries and ensure that all other details run smoothly?

Reception Site II | *Reception Site III*

Reception Site I

❧ Is there an on-site caterer? _____

❧ If not, are there kitchen facilities to
bring in an off-site caterer? _____

❧ Is there a particular caterer we are
required to use? _____

❧ Is there a particular florist or
photographer we must use? _____

❧ Are there rules regarding alcohol? _____

❧ Are there rules dictating style,
noise level, or the hours during
which music can be played? _____

❧ Is there enough space for a band or
disc jockey to set up? Where would
the band or disc jockey be? _____

❧ Is there a dance floor or enough space
to lay a rented floor? Where would
the dance floor be? _____

❧ What is the dance floor's capacity? _____

❧ Are there ample electrical outlets for
musical equipment? _____

❧ Are there any rules regarding
photography or videography? _____

❧ Are there any good spots for
formal pictures? _____

❧ Is there a good place to hold the
receiving line? _____

❧ Can we visit the site during another
event to see the space set up? _____

❧ Does your facility have any
decorations we can use? _____

❧ What is the parking capacity? _____

❧ Is the parking area located close to
the site's entrance? _____

❧ Is valet parking offered?
If so, what is the cost? _____

❧ If valet parking is not offered,
can we hire outside valet parkers? _____

Reception Site II | *Reception Site III*

Reception Site I

❦ Once inside, how are guests directed to the event? _____

❦ Where are the bathrooms located? _____

❦ How many stalls are there? _____

❦ Is there an attendant? At any additional cost to us? _____

❦ May we see the bathrooms? _____

❦ *If outdoors:* Is there room for portable toilets? _____

❦ Is there a coat room? _____

❦ Is there a coat room attendant? At any additional cost to us? _____

❦ Is there a place to set up a gift table? If so, do you provide the table? _____

❦ Is throwing birdseed or blowing bubbles allowed after the reception, and is there a place to do this? _____

❦ Is there a place to change into going-away outfits? _____

❦ Is there security on-site and in the parking lot? _____

❦ Do you have liability insurance? What are we responsible for? _____

❦ How much of a deposit is required? _____

❦ When is the balance due? _____

❦ What is your cancellation policy? _____

❦ Can you provide a list of references who have recently had weddings here? _____

❦ Other questions/notes: _____

Reception Site II	Reception Site III

Food

Facts at Your Fingertips: The Lingo

✧ **American service (also "plated service"):** Food is set on the plates in the kitchen, then brought out to seated guests. This is typically the most cost-efficient service style.

✧ **French service:** Traditionally, this style consisted of a six-member serving team who prepared meals tableside. Because this is an expensive endeavor, many caterers today simply incorporate some French-style touches; in such a case, food can be cooked in the kitchen and the final details, such as tossing salads or carving beef, attended to by the wait staff tableside. Food is served with two long serving forks.

✧ **Russian service:** Members of the wait staff serve each course from platters, placing the food on plates already set at guests' seats.

✧ **Family style:** Platters of food prepared in the kitchen are set at the table, and guests serve themselves. This style cuts back on the need for extensive wait staff, but makes it difficult to gauge the precise amount of food needed.

✧ **Corkage fee:** This is the fee caterers charge for opening a bottle of alcohol. When the bar tab is included in the catering fee, there is usually no corkage fee. If the bar is a separate tab or you'll be bringing in your own liquor, ask if there will be a corkage fee (and have the price stated in your contract).

Questions to Ask: Catering

Caterer I

Name:

Address:

Phone/Fax:

E-mail:

❤ How long have you been in business?

❤ What are some of the styles of weddings you have worked on in the past?

❤ Do you offer all types of service: seated, buffet, station, and cocktail?

Menu Checklist

(Use this list according to your specific needs.)

Cocktail hour
- ☐ bar
- ☐ hors d'oeuvres

Main reception
- ☐ Appetizer
- ☐ Salad
- ☐ Soup
- ☐ Entrée
- ☐ Cake
- ☐ Other desserts
- ☐ Bar/beverages
- ☐ Champagne toast

KEEP IN MIND

The wait staff/guest ratio is an important one. For a seated meal, it is best to have one server for every eight- to ten-person table. For a buffet, there should ideally be one waiter for every twenty-five people.

Caterer II   Caterer III

_____

_____

_____

_____

_____

_____

_____

_____

_____

_____

_____

Caterer I

❤ What is the service style for seated: French, Russian, or plated?

❤ *If on-site catering:* Who will be the chef on duty on our wedding day?

❤ Are there set menu packages, or can one be custom-made?

❤ What are menu suggestions that fit our budget, style, and season—for both the cocktail hour and dinner?

❤ Will guests be offered entrée options?

❤ Do you offer special meals (kosher, low-fat, vegetarian)? Are there any on hand for last-minute requests?

❤ How do you accommodate any last-minute changes?

❤ Will you/the chef prepare special family recipes?

❤ What are the fees, and what do they include?

❤ Are gratuities additional?

❤ Do you offer tastings to help select the menu?

❤ Is there an additional charge for tastings?

❤ Would the tastings be prepared by the same person doing the food for our wedding?

❤ Is a traditional wedding cake extra? And a groom's cake?

❤ If we contract the wedding cake from a private baker, do you charge a cake-cutting fee?

Caterer II	*Caterer III*

Caterer I

❤ Is champagne for a toast included?
If not, what is the charge?

❤ What do overtime charges include?

❤ When would they go into effect?

❤ Is there a minimum number of plates
that must be ordered?

❤ Can you explain the bar fees?

❤ Are bar fees based on consumption
or the number of opened bottles?

❤ What label of alcohol is used?

❤ Are sodas/tonics provided at no charge?

❤ Are refunds given for unopened bottles?

❤ Can we bring in our own liquor?

❤ Will you provide a shopping list if
we choose to bring in liquor?

❤ Is there a corkage fee?

❤ Do you offer meals for musicians/
photographers/videographers at
a lower price?

❤ Do you offer children's meals at a
lower price?

❤ Who will be overseeing the wait staff
and kitchen staff on our wedding day?

❤ How long has your staff worked
with you?

❤ How will the staff be dressed?

❤ What is the server/guest ratio?

❤ *If off-site caterer:* Have you worked at
our site? If so, does it meet your needs?
If you haven't worked at the site, will
you visit it to check out the facilities?

❤ Do you provide tables, chairs, linens,
china, glassware, serving pieces, etc.?
If so, is a security deposit required in
case of breakage or stains?

Caterer II

Caterer III

Caterer I

❤ If you don't provide these items,
do you work with a rental company
that offers discounts to your clients?

❤ Will you provide a list of rental
items needed?

❤ Will you be responsible for receiving
rental deliveries and organizing
rental returns?

❤ *If caterer is responsible for tables:*
How are the tables arranged?

❤ *If tables are provided by caterer:*
How many guests can sit comfortably
at each table?

❤ How are the setup and cleanup
handled?

❤ How many meetings can we plan to
have with you?

❤ When do you need the final head
count?

❤ Do you have liability insurance?

❤ How are you licensed?
Can we see your health permit?

❤ How much of a deposit is required?

❤ What is your cancellation policy?

❤ Do you have references?

❤ Other questions/notes:

Caterer II	Caterer III

The Cake

Facts at Your Fingertips: Cake Talk

✧ **Buttercream:** This versatile cake filling and frosting can be colored and flavored for a variety of effects. It can also be used for cake trimmings, such as beaded edgings and faux flowers. Made from a mixture of softened butter, milk or cream, confectioners' sugar, and egg yolks, buttercream does not hold up well in the heat and, hence, is not ideal for an outdoor summer wedding.

✧ **Fondant:** This malleable sugar, water, and cream of tartar mixture can be wrapped around a cake for a porcelain finish or molded into decorations, such as flowers, fruits, bows, and other fancy designs.

✧ **Royal icing:** Made from sugar and egg whites, this icing can be tinted any color and hardens when dry to make sturdy decorations for cakes.

✧ **Marzipan:** This almond paste, sugar, and egg white mixture can be tinted with food coloring and molded to make trimmings, such as flowers, fruits, bows, and other designs.

Questions to Ask: Cake

Bakery I

Company name:
Contact person:
Address:

Phone/Fax:
E-mail:

❧ Do you have a portfolio from which
   we can select a style?

❧ Will you create a custom design based
   on our vision?

❧ What are some flavor combinations
   you can suggest for fillings and icings?

❧ What are some cake trimmings you
   like to use?

> ### Keep in Mind
> It is not uncommon for the happy couple to eat very little during the reception. That said, put someone in charge of preparing a plate of food for the two of you to enjoy after the wedding.

Bakery II	Bakery III

Bakery I

❤ Have you worked with real flowers? _____

❤ Are you familiar with the safety issues _____
regarding edible flowers and the need _____
to use flowers free from pesticides? _____

❤ Have you worked with sugared fruits _____
and flowers? _____

❤ Do you offer a cake tasting? _____

❤ Is the cake prepared and then frozen, or _____
is it prepared fresh for the wedding day? _____

_____

❤ What is the fee? Is it based on a _____
per-person charge? _____

_____

_____

❤ Are delivery and setup included? _____
If not, what is the additional cost? _____

❤ Will you decorate a cake with faux _____
layers for display and prepare a less _____
expensive sheet cake for cutting and _____
serving? _____

❤ Will you do a groom's cake? If so, what _____
are our choices and what is the fee? _____

_____

_____

❤ How far in advance do we need _____
to place our order? _____

❤ Do you have references? _____

_____

_____

_____

_____

❤ Other questions/notes: _____

_____ _____

_____ _____

_____ _____

_____ _____

Bakery II	*Bakery III*

Wedding Consultant

What a wedding consultant can do:
✧ Plan the entire event, from finding the site to handling the details on the wedding day.
✧ Make arrangements for select aspects of the wedding, such as the flowers, music, and photography.
✧ Run the show on the wedding day only.

Why you might want to hire a wedding consultant:
✧ To save time. A consultant can take on a large or small amount of responsibility and also weed out some of the early search steps.
✧ To plan a long-distance event.
✧ To reap the rewards of consultant/vendor relationships and possible discounts.
✧ To gain the benefit of not starting from scratch. A consultant will know exactly what needs to be done and when and how to do it.
✧ To leave the worrying to a professional.
✧ To have a referee for family disputes.
✧ To obtain an unbiased professional opinion.
✧ To have someone on hand to deal with the details.
✧ To obtain the advice of someone knowledgeable about wedding etiquette. ⟶

Questions to Ask: Wedding Consultant

Wedding Consultant I

Name:
Address:

Phone/Fax:
E-mail:
❤ Do you have a portfolio with photos
    of weddings you've planned?
❤ Do you have a business license?
❤ How long have you been in business?
❤ Are you certified? By what association?

Why you might not want to hire a wedding consultant:

✧ Hiring a consultant can be pricey, and the cost might mean you can't afford something else you want.

✧ Hiring a stranger to help you plan one of the most personal days of your life might make you a bit more uncomfortable than you expected.

✧ It can be difficult to find just the right person to interpret your vision, and you may end up having to compromise on certain aspects.

✧ The person you choose may not be in sync with your groom or other family members, creating yet another "relationship" you need to be concerned about.

✧ Depending on your consultant's personality, you could feel as if you're losing control over your wedding.

Things to Do

☐ Interview potential candidates
☐ Book wedding consultant
☐ Schedule progress meetings
☐ Send signed contract and deposit to wedding consultant
☐ Confirm final details with wedding consultant
☐ Get contact number of wedding consultant for wedding day

Wedding Consultant II	*Wedding Consultant III*

Wedding Consultant I

❤ What is your fee? Do you charge hourly, a flat fee, or a percentage of the total wedding budget?

❤ Can we hire you to plan the entire event?

❤ Can we hire you to help with just some of the planning?

❤ Can we hire you to help on the wedding day only?

❤ What details do you handle?

❤ What details won't you handle?

❤ How many meetings should we plan to have?

❤ Can we conduct business by phone, fax, or e-mail?

❤ *If site has been selected:* Have you planned any weddings at our site before?

❤ *If site has been selected:* Do you know the catering manager/ events planner at our site?

❤ Do you have vendors you've worked with in the past?

❤ Are there a few that you like for each service or just one vendor for each?

❤ Do these service providers offer your clients discounts?

Wedding Consultant II	Wedding Consultant III

Wedding Consultant I

🖜 What would the process be for selecting and hiring vendors for our wedding?

🖜 Do you like to take complete control, or do you welcome our ideas and participation?

🖜 Will you be on hand the day of the wedding?

🖜 How many other events will you be organizing on that day?

🖜 How many people on your staff will be at the wedding?

🖜 How long has your staff worked with you?

🖜 How will you (and your staff) be dressed?

🖜 *If hiring consultant to be at wedding:* What happens if you are ill on our wedding day?

🖜 Do you require meals?

🖜 Will you travel if necessary?

🖜 Will there be additional expenses for parking and travel?

🖜 Do you have liability insurance?

🖜 Do you have references?

🖜 Other questions/notes:

Wedding Consultant II	Wedding Consultant III

Rentals
(for an at-home wedding or a site where items are not provided)

Rentals Worksheet
(Use this list according to your specific needs.)

Rental Item	Description	Cost/ item	Qty.	Total Cost
CEREMONY				
Chairs				
Canopy for altar				
Aisle runner (may be provided by florist)				
Other				
COCKTAIL HOUR				
Chairs				
Tables				
Linens				
China				
Flatware				
Glassware				
Serving pieces				
Decorative accessories				
Other				

Vendor I

Vendor II				Vendor III			
Description	Cost/ item	Qty.	Total Cost	Description	Cost/ item	Qty.	Total Cost

Rental Item	Description	Cost/item	Qty.	Total Cost
RECEPTION				
Tent				
Chairs				
Tables				
Linens				
China				
Flatware				
Glassware				
Serving pieces				
Decorative accessories				
Dance floor				
Heaters				
Lights				
Portable toilets				
Other				
TOTAL				

Vendor I

Vendor II				Vendor III			
Description	Cost/ item	Qty.	Total Cost	Description	Cost/ item	Qty.	Total Cost
TOTAL				TOTAL			

Questions to Ask: Rental Company

Rental Company I

Company name:

Contact person:

Address:

Phone/Fax:

E-mail:

❤ Can your inventory accommodate the
size of our guest list?

❤ Do you deliver?

❤ Will you ship to an out-of-town site?

❤ How far in advance can items be
delivered?

❤ How soon after the event can items
be picked up?

❤ Will we incur extra charges because
of off delivery dates? For example,
if items from a Saturday night wedding
are not picked up until Monday because
there is no service on Sunday, will we
be charged for that extra day?

❤ Do you offer selections in various
price ranges?

❤ Do you offer a variety of tent styles?

❤ Do you offer a variety of table shapes
and sizes?

❤ Do you offer a variety of chair styles?

❤ Do you offer table linens in different
fabrics and colors?

Rental Company II	Rental Company III

Rental Company I

❤ Do you offer china, flatware, glassware, and serving pieces in different patterns/colors?

❤ Do you offer any other items we need?

❤ Is there anyone on staff to help us achieve the look we want?

❤ Is there a minimum number of items that must be ordered?

❤ What are the fees for the items we want? *(Refer to the worksheet on page 56 to record fees.)*

❤ Is setup included?

❤ Is there breakage coverage?

❤ How does the payment schedule work?

❤ What is your cancellation policy?

❤ Is there an emergency contact for the wedding day in case items are not delivered or arrive damaged?

❤ Do you have liability insurance?

❤ Do you have references?

❤ Other questions/notes:

Rental Company II	Rental Company III

Notes

Chapter Three

Stationery

Stationery

Things to Do

- [ ] Speak to stationers about ideas and costs
- [ ] Order desired stationery items *(refer to the worksheet on page 68, and use it according to your own desires/needs)*
- [ ] Send deposit to stationer
- [ ] Give wording for invitation (and for any other items you're ordering) to stationer
- [ ] Review proofs for invitation and for any other applicable items
- [ ] Obtain addresses for everyone on guest list
- [ ] Call calligraphers to see work/discuss fees
- [ ] Book calligrapher, or recruit a talented friend for your calligraphy needs
- [ ] Send guest list (with addresses) and envelopes to person addressing invitations
- [ ] Send seating cards and/or table number cards to calligrapher, if applicable
- [ ] Purchase special stamps for response envelopes
- [ ] Assemble invitations and stuff envelopes
- [ ] Bring envelopes to post office to be hand-stamped
- [ ] Create guest list chart to record responses *(it is helpful to create a spreadsheet on the computer; be sure to include guests' entrée selections if necessary)*
- [ ] Purchase guest book
- [ ] Purchase pen for guest book
- [ ] Assign friend or family member to oversee guest book at wedding
- [ ] Follow up with invitees who haven't responded (about two weeks before wedding)
- [ ] Address wedding announcements
- [ ] Arrange for someone to send wedding announcements on the day of or the day after the wedding
- [ ] Other _____
- [ ] _____
- [ ] _____
- [ ] _____
- [ ] _____
- [ ] _____
- [ ] _____

Facts at Your Fingertips: Invitation Inserts

The following are inserts that can accompany the main wedding invitation:

✧ **Ceremony/reception card:** This is the most common invitation for guests who are asked to attend both the ceremony and the reception. If you're having an intimate ceremony with a smaller guest list than that of the reception, send separate ceremony and reception cards.

✧ **Response card:** Guests will use this card to let you know if they'll be attending your wedding. If you need guests to give you their entrée selections ahead of time, include their choices on the card.

✧ **Response envelope:** Guests will use this small, stamped envelope to return the response card. The envelope should be preaddressed to the wedding host.

✧ **Pew card:** This card is sent to family and friends who have special assigned seats at the ceremony. The card should read "Please present this card" and include the name of the location, the date, and the pew or row number.

✧ **Within-the-ribbon card:** This card serves the same purpose as a pew card, except that instead of designating a specific pew number, it will say "Within the ribbon," referring to a roped-off section of pews in the front.

✧ **Map/directions card:** Often the venue will provide this, but if you want to have the map and information printed to match the style of your invitation, a stationer can usually accommodate you.

✧ **Accommodations card:** This card can be included in the invitations of out-of-town guests to provide them with information regarding any hotels where you've held blocks of rooms. Include the hotel's telephone number. (You could, instead, send a separate letter ahead of the invitations providing this information, as well as details regarding local area attractions; this will give guests plenty of time to make their travel arrangements.)

✧ **Rain card:** If you're planning an outdoor wedding and have an alternate location booked for inclement weather, include that location's name and address on this card.

✧ **Parking card:** If you have arranged for special parking nearby or on-site with valet service, include this information on a card with the words "Please present this card to the parking attendant" as well as "Gratuities included," if applicable.

✧ **Tissue paper:** This thin sheet of tissue, once used to prevent the invitation ink from smudging, is still considered an elegant touch.

✧ **Inner envelope:** This envelope, which is slightly smaller than the mailing envelope, holds the invitation and all other components. The inner envelope should remain unsealed and be addressed with the guests' names. For a formal wedding, put the title and last name of each guest on this envelope. For a more casual tone, use only their first names.

Facts at Your Fingertips: Printing Primer

✧ **Engraving:** This technique, which uses a metal plate with die-cut letters, creates raised letters on the front of a piece of paper (and small indentations on the back). This method takes longer than others and is the most expensive.

✧ **Thermography:** Less expensive than engraving but offering a similar look, this technique creates letters with a heating process that combines ink and powder. The letters are raised on the front side of the paper, but the back of the paper is smooth.

✧ **Offset:** This technique uses an inked rubber cylinder to print on the paper. The look is less formal than engraving or thermography, and the process is less expensive.

✧ **Embossing:** This technique, which creates raised lettering, is usually "blind," meaning the letters or symbols are the same color as the paper but stand out in relief. The method is most often used for monograms, borders, or artwork on stationery pieces.

Words to the Wise

✧ Send save-the-date cards to out-of-town guests as early as six to nine months before the wedding.

✧ Mail invitations six to eight weeks before the wedding (the earlier the better during holiday seasons).

✧ Don't include registry information on the invitations; rely upon word of mouth.

✧ Before ordering table number cards to identify reception tables, find out if your reception site or caterer will provide these.

✧ Order extra envelopes (inner and outer) to allow for any addressing mistakes.

✧ With the exception of people's titles, when addressing invitations do not use abbreviations.

✧ Some couples choose to send formal wedding announcements to friends and relatives who were not invited to the wedding. These announcements should be mailed either on the day of the ceremony or the day after.

Stationery Worksheet

Stationery Item	Description	Cost/ item	Qty.	Total Cost
		Vendor I		
Wedding invitations				
Outer envelopes				
Inner envelopes				
Ceremony cards				
Reception cards				
Response cards				
Response envelopes				
Pew cards				
Within-the-ribbon cards				
Map/directions cards				
Accommodations cards				
Rain cards				
Parking cards				
Tissue paper				
Engagement announcements				
Save-the-date cards				

| Vendor II | | | | Vendor III | | | |
Description	Cost/ item	Qty.	Total Cost	Description	Cost/ item	Qty.	Total Cost

Stationery Item	Description	Vendor I		
		Cost/ item	Qty.	Total Cost
Rehearsal dinner invitations				
Ceremony programs				
Menu cards				
Seating cards				
Table number cards				
Thank-you notes				
At-home cards				
Wedding announcements				
Other				
TOTAL				

KEEP IN MIND

Thank-you notes for engagement gifts and wedding presents given before the wedding should be sent within two weeks of receipt. Traditional etiquette dictates that you take no longer than one month to send your notes of gratitude for wedding presents received on or after the wedding day, but modern practices have extended this period to two months. (For those presents received on the wedding day, the clock starts ticking upon your return from the honeymoon.)

| Vendor II | | | | | Vendor III | | | |
Description	Cost/ item	Qty.	Total Cost		Description	Cost/ item	Qty.	Total Cost
TOTAL					TOTAL			

Questions to Ask: Stationery

Stationer I

Company name:

Contact person:

Address:

Phone/Fax:

E-mail:

❤ What are our options regarding the different pieces that can make up the wedding invitation (inner envelopes, response cards, etc.), and how do they affect the cost?

❤ Can you print up additional pieces to include with the invitation, such as a map/directions card and an accommodations card?

❤ What are our printing options, and how do they affect the cost?

❤ What are our paper options (material, weight, color), and how do they affect the cost?

❤ What are our options in type style?

❤ Can we see samples of different printing techniques, paper styles, and type styles?

❤ When do we need to place an order?

❤ When would the invitations be ready?

❤ Do you address envelopes? If so, do you print or do calligraphy by hand?

❤ Is there an extra fee for addressing envelopes?

Stationer II	*Stationer III*

Stationer I

❤ If you don't do calligraphy, do you
work with someone who does?
Does he/she give discounts to
your customers?

❤ Do we assemble the invitations and
stuff envelopes ourselves?

❤ Do we stamp and send out invitations?

❤ What is the difference in cost, if any,
between ordering extra invitations
up front or after the initial order
has been placed?

❤ Can we order extra envelopes
(inner and outer) in case of
addressing mistakes?

❤ Can the envelopes be delivered before
the invitations are ready so the
calligrapher can get started?

❤ Will we be able to see a proof before
any pieces are printed?

❤ Will you be able to help us compose
the proper wording for our invitation?

❤ Can you advise us as to what
information we should (and shouldn't)
include on the invitation?

❤ Can you help us find a special emblem
to use on our stationery?

❤ What are the rules regarding a
monogram?

❤ How should we arrange our names
on thank-you notes?

❤ Have you ever printed a program for
our faith's service?

❤ What are the costs for the invitations
we are interested in? *(Refer to the
worksheet on page 68 to record costs.)*

❤ What is the payment policy?

❤ What is the cancellation policy?

Stationer II	Stationer III

❤ Other questions/notes *(if there are
any other stationery items, such as
those listed in this section's worksheet,
that you wish to order, be sure to
discuss them with the stationer)*:

Stationer I

_____

_____

_____

_____

_____

_____

_____

_____

_____

_____

Questions to Ask: Calligraphy

Name:
Address:

Phone/Fax:
E-mail:

❤ Can we see samples of your work?
❤ Do you do calligraphy by hand or
computer?
❤ Do you provide a menu of calligraphy
styles to choose from?
❤ What style would work best with
our invitation?
❤ What are your fees?
What do they include?

❤ Do you do outer and inner envelopes?
❤ Will you do pieces that can then be
printed from your artwork, such as
the invitations themselves, maps,
menus, etc.?

Calligrapher I

_____

_____

_____

_____

_____

_____

_____

_____

_____

_____

_____

_____

_____

_____

_____

_____

_____

_____

_____

_____

Stationer II   *Stationer III*

Calligrapher II   *Calligrapher III*

Calligrapher I

❤ Will you do table numbers and
seating cards or a seating chart?

❤ When do you need the list of guests
and addresses?
❤ Can you accommodate last-minute
invitations?
❤ How long after you receive the
materials can we expect to have
completed pieces?
❤ Do you have references?

❤ Other questions/notes:

_____

_____

_____

_____

_____

_____

KEEP IN MIND
Instead of having individual seating cards, some couples choose to
have a single seating chart that tells everyone where they'll be dining.
Such a chart can make an attractive accent when artistically designed.
Should you wish to incorporate this option into your festivities, ask
the calligraphers you interview whether they can create one.

Calligrapher II	*Calligrapher III*

Notes

Chapter Four

Music & Flowers

Ceremony Music

Things to Do

- [ ] Interview ceremony musicians
- [ ] Arrange to listen to performances
- [ ] Book ceremony musician(s)
- [ ] Send signed contract and deposit to musicians
- [ ] Select music for:
    - [ ] prelude
    - [ ] attendants' processional
    - [ ] bride's processional
    - [ ] ceremony
    - [ ] recessional
    - [ ] postlude
- [ ] Give any necessary sheet music to musicians
- [ ] Make any necessary arrangements for equipment required by musicians
- [ ] Confirm date/times/location with musicians
- [ ] Get contact numbers of musicians for wedding day
- [ ] Other _____
- [ ] _____
- [ ] _____
- [ ] _____
- [ ] _____
- [ ] _____
- [ ] _____

Questions to Ask: Ceremony Music

Ceremony Musician I

Name: _____

Address: _____

_____

_____

Phone/Fax: _____

E-mail: _____

❤ What instrument(s) do you (and your
   co-performers) play? _____

❤ What is in your repertoire? _____

_____

_____

❤ Will you learn new pieces? _____

❤ Can you suggest pieces that will fit
   our wedding style? _____

_____

_____

_____

❤ Do you know the religious songs
   we want played? _____

❤ Have you performed at our site? _____

   If so, do you require any amplification?

   Provided by whom? _____

❤ If you're not familiar with the site,
   will you visit to assess the acoustics? _____

❤ If you're ill on our wedding day,
   do you have a backup? _____

❤ Can we meet/hear him or her? _____

❤ What will your attire be? _____

❤ Do you have liability insurance? _____

❤ What is your fee? _____

_____

❤ How much of a deposit do you require? _____

❤ When is the balance due? _____

❤ What is your cancellation policy? _____

_____

Ceremony Musician II	Ceremony Musician III

❤ Do you have references?

Ceremony Musician I

_____
_____
_____
_____
_____
_____

❤ Other questions/notes:

_____   _____
_____   _____
_____   _____

Reception Music

Things to Do

- [ ] Interview bands or disc jockeys
- [ ] Listen to bands/disc jockeys perform
- [ ] Book band/disc jockey
- [ ] Send contract and deposit to band/disc jockey
- [ ] Arrange to have music for:
    - [ ] cocktail hour
    - [ ] interlude between cocktail hour and main reception
    - [ ] introduction of married couple
    - [ ] first dance
    - [ ] father–daughter dance
    - [ ] mother–son dance
    - [ ] dinner
    - [ ] general dancing
    - [ ] traditional/religious dances
    - [ ] cake-cutting
    - [ ] bouquet toss
    - [ ] bride and groom's exit
- [ ] Arrange for band/disc jockey to see site and check facilities
- [ ] Give band the sheet music for songs you want them to learn

Ceremony Musician II	*Ceremony Musician III*

☐ Make any necessary arrangements for equipment required by band/disc jockey
☐ Give band/disc jockey list of requested songs and songs you don't want played
☐ Confirm date, times, and location with band/disc jockey
☐ Give schedule of events to band/disc jockey (include any announcements to be made, such as telling guests to pick up favors)
☐ Give any necessary compact discs to disc jockey
☐ Get contact numbers of musicians/disc jockey for wedding day
☐ Other _____
☐ _____
☐ _____

Words to the Wise

✧ It is a good idea to see any bands/disc jockeys that you are considering perform live at an event similar to yours; that way, you can get a feel for their style, the quality of their work, and the overall impression that they make.

✧ When selecting music, consider including a range of songs (from standards to current party hits) so there is something for everyone.

✧ Discuss where in the reception space the band or disc jockey will be stationed and where the speakers will be; you don't want the performers and their equipment to be too close to the reception tables, especially those where older guests are seated.

Questions to Ask: Band

Band I

Name:
Address:

Phone/Fax:
E-mail:
💙 What is your musical style?

💙 Can you play all different styles?
💙 Will you provide a song list to
choose from?
💙 Will you take requests from us of
songs to play and not to play?
💙 Will you take requests from guests?
💙 Will you learn new songs? How many?
💙 Do you know the traditional/ethnic
songs we want played?
💙 Will you be the master of ceremonies
(announcing the first dance, toasts,
cake-cutting, etc.)?
💙 What is your fee?

💙 How many hours does that include?
Of playing time? Of setting up and
breaking down equipment?
💙 How many pieces/what instruments
does that include?
💙 How many breaks (and of what length)
do you require?
💙 Will all the members take a break
at the same time, or will you rotate
so there is always live music?
💙 Will there be recorded music during
the break(s)?

Band II	Band III

Band I

- Will you play overtime?
- What is your overtime charge?
- Do you charge for travel time and parking?
- Do you have a demo tape?
- Can we see you perform live at an event?
- *If booking through an agency:* Will the musicians we hear on tape/ at a performance be the ones at our wedding?
- Have you played at our site before? If not, will you check out the site ahead of time?
- Does our site have the facilities (space, electrical capabilities) you need?
- If anything extra is required, is it our cost to incur or yours?
- Do you use any special lighting?
- Will any band members play at the ceremony, too?

- Is there an additional fee or a discount?

- Will any band members play during the cocktail hour?

- Is there an additional fee or a discount?

- Do you motivate the crowd, or do you limit your talking to emceeing duties?
- Do you have any group dances or contests in your repertoire? Will you refrain from doing these if we wish?
- What will your attire be?
- Do you require meals?
- When would you arrive to set up?

Band II	Band III

Band I

 Do you have another event the
same day?

 Do you have liability insurance?

 How much of a deposit is required?

 When is the balance due?

 What is your cancellation policy?

 Do you have references?

 Other questions/notes:

KEEP IN MIND

In preparation for your first dance, when all eyes will be focused on
you, you may want to take dancing lessons with your groom. Such
lessons can not only help you to dazzle guests with your grace and
style, but also give you an opportunity to spend some extra time with
your future husband.

Band II

Band III

Questions to Ask: Disc Jockey

Disc Jockey I

Name: _____

Address: _____
_____
_____

Phone/Fax: _____

E-mail: _____

❤ Do you have the types of music we're
looking for in your collection? _____
_____

❤ Are you willing to play songs that are
not in your collection? Will you obtain
those CDs, or must we provide them? _____

❤ Do you have the traditional/ethnic
songs we want? _____
_____

❤ Will you provide a song list to
choose from? _____

❤ Will you take requests from us of
songs to play and not to play? _____

❤ Will you take requests from guests? _____

❤ Will you be the master of ceremonies
(announcing the first dance, toasts,
cake-cutting, etc.)? _____

❤ What is your fee? _____

❤ How many hours does that include?
Of playing time? Of setting up and
breaking down equipment? _____

❤ How many breaks (and of what length)
do you require? _____

❤ Will music play during the break(s)? _____

❤ Will you play overtime? _____

❤ What is your overtime charge? _____

❤ Do you charge for travel time
and parking? _____

❤ Will you play during the cocktail hour? _____

❤ Is there an additional fee or a discount? _____

Disc Jockey II	Disc Jockey III

Disc Jockey I

❤ Can we see you in action at an event? _____

❤ *If booking through an agency:* _____
   Will the deejay we see on tape/at _____
   an event be the one at our wedding? _____

❤ Have you played at our site before? _____
   If not, will you check out the site _____
   ahead of time? _____

❤ Does the site have the facilities _____
   (space/electrical capabilities) you need? _____

❤ If anything extra is required, is it our _____
   cost to incur or yours? _____

❤ Do you use any special lighting? _____

❤ Do you motivate the crowd, or do you _____
   limit any talking to emceeing duties? _____

❤ Do you have any group dances or _____
   contests in your repertoire? Will you _____
   refrain from doing these if we wish? _____

❤ What will your attire be? _____

❤ Do you require a meal? _____

❤ When would you arrive to set up? _____

❤ Do you have another event the _____
   same day? _____

❤ Do you have liability insurance? _____

❤ How much of a deposit is required? _____

❤ When is the balance due? _____

❤ What is your cancellation policy? _____

❤ Do you have references? _____
   _____
   _____
   _____
   _____
   _____

❤ Other questions/notes: _____
_____ _____
_____ _____
_____ _____

Disc Jockey II	Disc Jockey III

Notes

Flowers

Things to Do

- [ ] Save photos/magazine clippings of flowers and arrangements for inspiration
- [ ] Make appointments to interview florists
- [ ] Hire florist
- [ ] Make appointment to see sample bouquets and arrangements
- [ ] Give table size to florist (so that centerpieces can be sized accordingly)
- [ ] Give florist swatches of dresses/table linens (to achieve complementary bouquets/arrangements)
- [ ] Make selections for all floral items *(see worksheet on page 98)*
- [ ] Send deposit to florist
- [ ] Send signed contract to florist
- [ ] Give measurement for length of aisle to florist if he/she is providing runner
- [ ] Confirm final details with florist
- [ ] Confirm date, times, and locations with florist
- [ ] Get contact number of florist for wedding day
- [ ] Other _____
- [ ] _____
- [ ] _____

Words to the Wise

✧ Bring pictures of floral arrangements and bouquets that you like to your interviews with florists; it is much easier to convey your ideas with visual aids.

✧ Make sure that centerpieces do not obstruct guests' views of one another.

✧ Avoid flowers with powerful scents, as they may interfere with your guests' enjoyment of the food.

✧ Discuss the staying power of the flowers you're interested in with your florist; you don't want your beautiful blooms to wilt halfway through the event. (Along these lines, you might want to include a statement in your contract that arrangements will consist of flowers in full bloom as well as buds that will bloom throughout the day.)

✧ Ask your attendants if they are allergic to any flowers; you don't want your bridesmaids to be sneezing when standing up for you.

✧ If you're planning on doing the bouquet toss but want to save your bridal bouquet, order a toss bouquet—a smaller bouquet intended specifically for this custom.

✧ Find out if the florist will dry your bouquet for a keepsake, or assign someone the task of attending to it while you're on your honeymoon.

Flower Worksheet

Element	Description	Cost/item	Qty.	Total Cost
	Vendor I			
PERSONAL FLOWERS				
Bride's bouquet				
Maid of honor's bouquet				
Bridesmaids' bouquets				
Groom's boutonniere				
Groomsmen's boutonnieres				
Special people corsages				
Special people boutonnieres				
Floral hair accessories				
Flower girls' baskets				
Toss bouquet				
Other				
CEREMONY SITE FLOWERS/ACCESSORIES				
Entryway				
Altar				
Aisles				
Huppah or wedding canopy				

	Vendor II					Vendor III		
Description	Cost/ item	Qty.	Total Cost		Description	Cost/ item	Qty.	Total Cost

Element	Description	Vendor I		
		Cost/ item	Qty.	Total Cost
Rose petals to sprinkle down aisle				
Program table				
Guest book table				
Cloth aisle runner (often supplied by florist)				
Candles				
Other				
RECEPTION FLOWERS				
Dinner tables (centerpieces and/or individual blooms at place settings)				
Dinner buffet tables/serving stations				
Cocktail hour guest tables				
Cocktail hour buffet tables				
Entryway				
Seating card table				
Favor table				
Cake table				
Gift table				
Rest rooms				
Favors for guests				
TOTAL				

Vendor II				Vendor III			
Description	Cost/ item	Qty.	Total Cost	Description	Cost/ item	Qty.	Total Cost
TOTAL				TOTAL			

Questions to Ask: Flowers

Florist I

Name:

Address:

Phone/Fax:

E-mail:

- Can we see photos of weddings you've done?
- Do you have one particular style, or will you work with us to create arrangements that match our vision?
- Will you look at pictures we've found to help explain what we want?
- Can we see sample arrangements?
- Do you specialize in weddings?
- What other types of events have you done?
- Have you done any events at our site?
- Where do you get the flowers for the arrangements?
- Are arrangements made the day of or before? How are they stored?

- Will you be on hand on the wedding day arranging and setting up, or will someone else be doing this?
- If someone else, can we see this person's work and meet him/her?
- Do you provide an aisle runner for the ceremony?
- Do you provide candles and create displays with them?
- Can you build a wedding canopy or huppah?

Florist II	Florist III

Florist I

❧ Can you work with our cake decorator
if we want flowers on the cake? Are
you familiar with the safety issues
regarding edible flowers and the need
to use flowers free from pesticides?

❧ Do you do floral favors?

❧ What will the costs be for the different
elements we are interested in?
(Refer to the worksheet on page 98
to record costs.)

❧ Can you suggest some money-saving
strategies?

❧ Will the flowers we're interested
in be in season at the time of our
wedding? If not, can you suggest
some similar-looking alternatives
to save money?

❧ How do you feel about transforming
pew arrangements from the ceremony
into centerpieces for the reception to
help ease our budget?

❧ Are there delivery and setup fees?

❧ Are the centerpiece vases ours to keep,
or do they need to go back to you?

❧ How many planning meetings should
we expect to have?

❧ How many other events are you
scheduled to work on our wedding day?

❧ What time would the flowers be
delivered, and when would you
(and your team) arrive to set up?

Florist II	*Florist III*

Florist I

 Do you have liability insurance?

 How much of a deposit do you require?

 When is the balance due?

 What is your cancellation policy?

 Do you have references?

 Other questions/notes:

KEEP IN MIND
If the vases do not need to go back to the florist, you may want to offer your centerpieces to guests as favors or donate the arrangements to a local hospital or nursing home.

Florist II	Florist III

Notes

Chapter Five

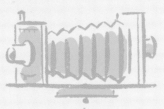

Photography &
Videography

Photography

Things to Do

- [ ] Look through wedding albums of family members and friends to get a sense of the photography style you want
- [ ] Make appointments to interview photographers
- [ ] Book photographer
- [ ] Send signed contract and deposit to photographer
- [ ] Make appointment for engagement picture sitting
- [ ] Scout potential photo spots—at home, at a local park, at wedding location
- [ ] Give photographer list of desired shots and important people to be photographed *(see page 195 for sample list)*
- [ ] Assign attendant to point out important people to photographer
- [ ] Give a copy of shot list to said attendant
- [ ] Select albums (including page and border style)
- [ ] Confirm details with photographer
- [ ] Get contact number from photographer for wedding day
- [ ] Purchase disposable cameras for tables
- [ ] Assign someone to put disposable cameras on tables
- [ ] Other _____

Words to the Wise

✧ When meeting with a photographer, ask to see an album of one entire wedding; if you review a portfolio that contains shots from different weddings, you are seeing only the best couple of shots from each event and you're not necessarily getting a realistic view of the photographer's ability.

✧ If you're booking a photographer through an agency, make sure that the photographer who will be shooting your wedding is the one whose work you've reviewed. And be sure to meet the photographer in person.

✧ Before the wedding day, scout out your location (and have your photographer do the same) to determine the best settings for photographs; you don't want to waste precious time on the day of your big event fretting about where to pose.

✧ To play it safe, make sure your photographer brings backup equipment; that way, you won't be left without any pictures of this momentous occasion if something malfunctions.

✧ Consider taking some, if not all, formal portraits before the ceremony to avoid spending valuable reception time posing for the camera. If you don't want your groom to see you before the ceremony, arrange to do only those shots that don't include the two of you.

Questions to Ask: Photography

Photographer I

Name:

Address:

Phone/Fax:

E-mail:

💌 What is your style?

💌 Do you prefer formal portraits, candids, or a combination?

💌 Do you shoot weddings primarily?

💌 What other types of photography have you done?

💌 Can we see a portfolio of your work?

💌 Can we see an album of one entire wedding?

💌 Can we see indoor and outdoor shots?

💌 What is your fee?

💌 For how many hours?

💌 How many shots will be taken?

💌 How many proofs will we see?

💌 How many albums are included in the cost?

💌 What is the cost for additional albums?

💌 How many shots in each album?

💌 Are all the album shots the same size?

💌 Can we add pages to an album, and if so, what is the cost?

💌 How many portraits are included in the fee?

💌 What are our size options for portraits (8×10, 5×7, 5×5, wallet, etc.)?

💌 What is the cost for additional prints?

Photographer II	Photographer III

Photographer I

❤ Do we get to keep the proofs and/or negatives as part of the package? If not, can we purchase them or do you always own them?

❤ If you keep the negatives, for how long do you save them?

❤ What kind of camera do you use?

❤ What quality and brand of film/paper do you use?

❤ Are album pages acid-free/archival quality?

❤ Do we have choices for album, page, and border styles?

❤ Can we see our album options?

❤ Is there an extra fee to have our names and wedding date printed on the cover of the album?

❤ Do you develop the film or send it to a lab?

❤ Are the photos we looked at developed by the same person/lab who would be doing ours?

❤ Do you retouch images?

❤ Do you bring backup equipment?

❤ Have you worked at our site before?

❤ Do you know good places for shots?

❤ If you're unfamiliar with our site, are you willing to visit it and scout for shot locations?

❤ Will you shoot the rehearsal and rehearsal dinner? What would the fee be?

❤ Will you come early on the day of the wedding to take shots of us getting ready? Is this included in the fee for the wedding, or is this extra?

Photographer II

Photographer III

Photographer I

❤ How long should formal pictures take? _____

❤ Will you work off a prepared shot list? _____

❤ If you take table shots, must we order
all of them? _____

❤ Will you shoot black-and-white
as well as color? _____

❤ How many photographers and
assistants will be there? _____

❤ If others will be shooting photos,
can we see their work? _____

❤ If you're ill, who will photograph our
wedding? _____

❤ How long after the wedding will we
see proofs? _____

❤ How long after we make our proof
selections will we receive the prints
and/or albums? _____

❤ What will your attire be? _____

❤ Do you require meals? _____

❤ Are there any additional charges
(e.g., parking, travel)? _____

❤ How much of a deposit is required? _____

❤ When is the balance due? _____

❤ What is your cancellation policy? _____

❤ Do you have liability insurance? _____

❤ Do you have references? _____

❤ Other questions/notes: _____

Photographer II	*Photographer III*

Videography

Things to Do

- [ ] Watch wedding videos of family and friends to determine desired style
- [ ] Make appointments to interview videographers
- [ ] Book videographer
- [ ] Send signed contract and deposit to videographer
- [ ] Give videographer list of desired shots and important people *(use sample list on page 195 as a guide)*
- [ ] Assign attendant to point out important people to videographer
- [ ] Give shot list to said attendant
- [ ] Confirm details with videographer
- [ ] Get contact number from videographer for wedding day
- [ ] Other _____
- [ ] _____
- [ ] _____
- [ ] _____

Questions to Ask: Videography

Videographer I

Name: _____

Address: _____

_____

_____

Phone/Fax: _____

E-mail: _____

❤ What is your filming style? _____

_____

❤ Do you have a tape for us to view? _____

❤ Can we see a tape of a wedding similar to ours? _____

❤ Have you shot indoors and outdoors, by candlelight and twilight? _____

❤ Do you shoot weddings primarily? _____

Facts at Your Fingertips: Videography Terms

◇ **Highlights tape:** Typically included in basic packages, this five- to ten-minute video is a wrap-up of the high points of your wedding in chronological order. It can be set to music (the song for your first dance, perhaps) and may include special visual effects.

◇ **Documentary style (short-form):** This video style, often shot in black-and-white, involves shooting hours of straight coverage and then editing it down for a tape of an agreed-upon length (often one hour) while still keeping the story and feeling intact.

◇ **Straight-cut format:** Just as it sounds, this style entails shooting your wedding from start to finish with little, if any, editing. The video may be long, but you won't have missed a thing.

◇ **In-camera style:** The videographer shoots just certain moments of the wedding.

KEEP IN MIND

After you've received your wedding video, be sure to remove the appropriate tab at the edge of the cassette so that you don't accidentally tape over this special feature presentation.

Videographer II	Videographer III

Videographer I

- What other types of videography have you done?
- What is your fee?

- How many hours of service and raw footage does that include?
- How many tapes of what length does that include?
- What is the cost of additional tapes?

- Is the final copy uncut or edited?
- If edited, who does the editing?
- Can we see some of his/her work?
- Do we help edit, or do you decide what to cut?
- If we're getting an edited tape, what happens to the raw footage?
- Is a shorter highlights tape included in the fee?
- What kind of special effects can we include? Is there an additional cost?

- How do you transition between scenes?

- Can you lay music over some scenes? Is there an additional cost?
- Can you do titles? Is there an additional cost?
- Can we provide baby photos and honeymoon photos to be incorporated into the video? Is there an extra cost?
- Will you work off a shot list?
- Have you shot at our wedding site?
- Do you know good places at our site to shoot?

Videographer II	*Videographer III*

Videographer I

❤ Will you come early to shoot us getting
  ready and having formal pictures taken?
  If so, is there an additional cost?

❤ Do you shoot in black-and-white and
  color?

❤ What type of equipment do you use?

❤ Is it portable?

❤ Do you bring backup equipment?

❤ Can you be inconspicuous during the
  ceremony and reception?

❤ How many videographers and
  assistants will be there?

❤ If others will be shooting footage,
  can we see their work?

❤ If you're ill on the wedding day,
  who will take your place?

❤ When will we receive the video(s)?

❤ What will your attire be?

❤ Do you require meals?

❤ Do you have liability insurance?

❤ Are there any other charges
  (e.g., parking, travel)?

❤ How much of a deposit is required?

❤ When is the balance due?

❤ What is your cancellation policy?

❤ Do you have references?

❤ Other questions/notes:

Videographer II	Videographer III

Notes

Chapter Six

Fashion

Bridal Attire

Things to Do

- [ ] Clip photos of dress styles you like from magazines
- [ ] Make appointments at bridal salons
- [ ] Ask parent or maid of honor to accompany you to bridal salons
- [ ] Select:
  - [ ] gown
  - [ ] veil/headpiece
  - [ ] blusher veil
  - [ ] shoes (before first fitting)
  - [ ] undergarments appropriate for gown (before first fitting)
  - [ ] hosiery (have extra pairs on hand on wedding day)
  - [ ] garter
  - [ ] earrings
  - [ ] necklace
  - [ ] other jewelry
  - [ ] hair accessories
  - [ ] purse
  - [ ] wrap
  - [ ] gloves
  - [ ] going-away outfit
  - [ ] rehearsal dinner outfit
- [ ] Schedule gown fittings
- [ ] Find out what you need to bring to fittings
- [ ] Obtain swatches of gown for florist and professional who will be dyeing shoes
- [ ] Discuss bustle style of train with seamstress
- [ ] Bring parent or maid of honor to fitting to learn how to bustle train
- [ ] Find out from bridal salon how to hang and care for dress
- [ ] Find out from bridal salon what to do if dress is wrinkled before wedding
- [ ] Find out from bridal salon what to do if you get a spot on the dress

If borrowing a gown:
- [ ] Take gown out of storage
- [ ] Determine what alterations, if any, are needed
- [ ] Examine gown for stains and rips
- [ ] Take gown to reputable seamstress for alterations (if an older gown, take to a professional equipped to handle vintage garments)
- [ ] Take gown to reputable professional for cleaning and/or steaming

- [ ] Plan time and place to bustle gown after ceremony
- [ ] Arrange for place to store going-away outfits at reception site
- [ ] Arrange for place to change into going-away outfits
- [ ] Take shoes to be dyed to match gown
- [ ] Pick up dyed shoes
- [ ] Pick up gown
- [ ] Break in shoes and scuff shoe bottoms (so that they're comfortable and you don't slip in them)
- [ ] Find professional dry cleaner who specializes in bridal gown care to clean and pack up dress and accessories after wedding
- [ ] Assign someone to take wedding gown home for you after wedding (if you won't be able to do so yourself)
- [ ] Assign someone to take gown to dry cleaner after wedding
- [ ] Other _____
- [ ] _____
- [ ] _____
- [ ] _____
- [ ] _____
- [ ] _____
- [ ] _____

Words to the Wise

✧ Most bridal salons require appointments, so call before visiting one.

✧ If making an appointment on the weekend, request an early time slot or be prepared for long waits.

✧ Try on a variety of dress styles; something that looks great on the hanger may not be flattering when you put it on, and something that you never thought you'd consider might look fabulous.

✧ Make sure that you feel comfortable in the gown that you select; you don't want to be tugging at the dress or worrying that you don't look your best on your wedding day.

✧ Before purchasing a gown, inquire as to whether or not the salon carries any insurance and what exactly that insurance covers; if the store doesn't have insurance, you are running the risk of losing your money if the place goes out of business or if your dress is ruined by a fire or flood while in the store's possession.

✧ Once you've selected a gown, ask the sales associate for recommendations regarding undergarments.

Facts at Your Fingertips: Silhouettes

◇ **Ball gown:** Exuding a timeless romantic quality, this dress boasts a full skirt that springs from a fitted waist.

◇ **A-line/princess:** Admired for its clean lines and soft yet angular form, this subdued variation of the ball gown features a slightly tapered waist that gives way to a gentle A-shaped skirt.

◇ **Empire:** This high-waisted dress, beloved for its period look, features a straight column or A-line skirt flowing from just below the bustline.

◇ **Slip dress:** Designed with simple spaghetti straps, a low-cut neckline (typically a scoop or V neck), and unembellished fabric, this style is chosen by brides who want to make a quietly elegant statement.

◇ **Sheath:** This straight, modern-looking style comes in a little at the waist before hitting the floor in one clean, sleek column.

Questions to Ask: When Making Bridal Salon Appointments

Salon I

Salon name: _____

Address: _____

_____

_____

Phone: _____

 Do I need an appointment to see and try on dresses? _____

 What is the price range of the dresses? _____

 How long does it take to order a gown? _____

 Will I be assigned a sales associate, or will I try on gowns on my own? _____

 Will I be able to look at your collection of gowns and select what I'd like to try on, or will a sales associate be deciding what to show and not show me? _____

 Can I bring pictures of gowns I've seen so you can tell me if you carry them or so you can get an idea of what I like? _____

 Is there a limit to how many dresses I can try on? _____

 Do you hold designer trunk shows? _____

 Do I need to bring special undergarments and shoes to try on dresses, or do you provide these? _____

KEEP IN MIND

If you are planning to have shoes dyed to match your gown, make sure the shoes you select are dyeable.

Salon II	Salon III

Questions to Ask: Wedding Gown

Salon I

Salon name: _____

Sales associate: _____

Address: _____

_____

_____

Phone/Fax: _____

E-mail: _____

❤ What style of dress do you recommend _____
for my body type? _____

❤ Are some styles better for certain _____
seasons? _____

❤ Are some fabrics better for certain _____
seasons? _____

❤ Can any of the designs I try on be _____
customized? _____

❤ Are some dress designs available in _____
more than one fabric (i.e., are there _____
less expensive yet similar fabric _____
alternatives for some dresses)? _____

❤ Do dresses come in more than one _____
color (e.g., choice of white or ivory)? _____

❤ How much is the gown I'm _____
interested in? _____

_____

_____

_____

❤ What does the gown price include? _____

❤ Are alterations extra? _____

❤ How many fittings will there be? _____

❤ Do you steam the dress after final _____
alterations? _____

❤ Do you sell accessories such as veils, _____
shoes, and hosiery? *(Costs can be* _____
recorded in the space provided at _____
the end of this list of questions.) _____

Salon II	Salon III

Salon 1

❤️ If you don't sell accessories, do you have discount relationships with stores that do?

❤️ Can you recommend someone to dye shoes to match the gown?

❤️ How far in advance of the wedding will the dress be ready?

❤️ Do you deliver?

❤️ Can I hire someone to bustle me after the ceremony? What is the fee?

❤️ Do you handle care for the gown after the wedding, or can you recommend a reputable wedding gown cleaner/preserver?

❤️ Do you offer discounts for bridesmaid dresses if I purchase my gown here?

❤️ How long has this salon been in business?

❤️ Do you carry any type of insurance? What does it cover?

❤️ How much of a deposit is required?

❤️ When is the balance due?

❤️ Do you accept credit cards?

❤️ What is the cancellation policy?

❤️ Accessory costs:

❤️ Other questions/notes:

Salon II	Salon III

Notes

Bridal Attendants' Attire

Things to Do

- [ ] Make appointments to see bridesmaid dresses
- [ ] Select dresses
- [ ] Give attendants' measurements to salon, or have attendants do so
- [ ] Give any necessary contact information for attendants to salon, or have attendants do so
- [ ] Arrange to have dresses for out-of-town attendants sent to them, or have attendants do so
- [ ] Obtain swatches of the bridesmaid dresses to show florist (for bouquets/arrangements) and professional who will be dyeing shoes
- [ ] If attendants are selecting their own dresses in a color of your choosing, send swatches of the color to attendants
- [ ] If attendants are not having alterations done at the same place, give them instructions as to where the hemline should fall
- [ ] Select shoes for attendants, or give them guidelines for doing so
- [ ] Select any accessories for attendants (purse, gloves, jewelry)
- [ ] Select attire for child attendants, or give their parents guidelines for doing so
- [ ] Follow up with attendants to make sure that they have their attire and accessories ready for the wedding day
- [ ] Other _____
- [ ] _____
- [ ] _____

Words to the Wise

✧ When ordering bridesmaid dresses, make sure that there is plenty of time to have alterations done after the garments' scheduled arrival date.

✧ Be considerate of your bridesmaids' feelings by selecting a style that is flattering on all of them; toward the same end, and for a little variety, you could have your attendants wear different styles in the same color.

✧ For your bridesmaids' gifts, consider purchasing something that the attendants can wear to the wedding—such as earrings or a necklace.

✧ Traditionally, bridesmaids pay for their own attire. Some brides choose to make a contribution to this expense.

✧ Don't feel that you must order bridesmaid dresses from a salon. It is perfectly acceptable to select off-the-rack dresses.

Questions to Ask: Bridal Attendants' Attire

Salon I

Salon name:

Sales associate:

Address:

Phone/Fax:

E-mail:

- ❤ What styles do you recommend for a group with different sizes/body types?
- ❤ How do you handle dress orders and fittings for out-of-town bridesmaids? Do you have pictures or sketches of dresses to send them?
- ❤ Can you ship?
- ❤ How far in advance do we need to order the dresses?
- ❤ How long after we place the order will the dresses arrive?
- ❤ *If there's a discount because you bought wedding dress at same store:* If my bridesmaids order different dress styles, will there still be a discount?
- ❤ What is the price of the dress?

- ❤ Do you do alterations? If not, do you work with someone who offers your customers a discount?
- ❤ If you do alterations, are they included in the cost of the dress? If alterations are not included, what is the cost?
- ❤ How much is shipping?
- ❤ Do you carry any insurance? What does it cover?
- ❤ How much of a deposit is required?
- ❤ When is the balance due?

Salon II	Salon III

Salon I

❤ What is your cancellation policy?

_____

❤ Other questions/notes:

_____

_____   _____

_____   _____

_____   _____

_____   _____

Groom's and Groomsmen's Attire

(You may want to photocopy the following section for your husband-to-be.)

Things to Do

☐ Decide upon the style of tuxedo/suit (often determined by the time and formality of the wedding)

☐ Call formalwear stores to see if you need an appointment and if you need to bring anything

☐ Try on ensembles

☐ Purchase tuxedo/suit or book rental

☐ Select:

    ☐ shirt

    ☐ shoes

    ☐ tie

    ☐ cumberbund/vest

    ☐ pocket square

    ☐ cuff links

    ☐ tie clip

    ☐ studs

    ☐ socks

☐ Organize groomsmen's attire (refer to checklist above for ensemble components)

☐ Obtain measurements for out-of-town groomsmen

☐ Select going-away ensemble

☐ Pick up tuxedo/suit

☐ Assign someone to return tuxedo if a rental

☐ Other _____

☐ _____

Salon II	*Salon III*

Words to the Wise

✧ The groom might want to consider purchasing a tuxedo rather than renting one; by figuring out how much use he would get out of a tuxedo and looking into the costs of renting and buying, he will be able to make an informed decision that could save money in the long run.

✧ If the groom doesn't wish to wear a tuxedo, and you're not planning a formal evening wedding, discuss opting for a dark suit. For a more casual affair, an ensemble consisting of neutral trousers and a dark blazer is a possibility.

✧ If renting, the groom and groomsmen should pick up their tuxedos a few days before the wedding so that there's time to fix any problems that might arise (the wrong tux was ordered, it doesn't fit properly, etc.).

✧ Men should wear either a boutonniere or a pocket square—not both.

Questions to Ask: Groom's Attire

(The following questions can be used in the search for the groomsmen's attire, too.)

Store I

Store name: _____
Sales associate: _____
Address: _____
_____
_____

Phone/Fax: _____
E-mail: _____

If renting:

❤ How far in advance do I need to reserve the rental? _____

❤ What are the different styles that you offer? _____

❤ How old is the formalwear you rent out? _____

❤ Will I be able to see/examine the actual suit that I will be getting? _____

❤ What is included as part of the package? _____

❤ What is the cost? _____

❤ How do fittings/alterations work? Are they included in the cost or extra? _____

❤ When can I pick up the ensemble? _____

❤ Is the ensemble cleaned and pressed before pickup? _____

❤ When is the ensemble due back? _____

❤ Will I incur extra charges if the tuxedo gets stained, or do you assume there will be some amount of wear and tear? _____

Store II	Store III

Store I

💕 Do you offer discounts for ushers if I rent my attire from your store?

💕 How much of a deposit is required?

💕 When is the balance due?

💕 What is the cancellation policy?

If buying:

💕 How far in advance of the wedding do I need to place my order?

💕 What is included in the price?

💕 Are alterations extra?

💕 How many fittings will there be?

💕 Is there anything I need to bring to the fittings?

💕 Do you sell shoes and accessories?

💕 If not, do you have discount relationships with stores that sell shoes and accessories?

💕 Do you offer rentals for ushers?

💕 Do you carry insurance? What does it cover?

💕 What is the cost of the tuxedo/suit I'm interested in?

💕 When would the tuxedo/suit be ready?

💕 How much of a deposit is required?

💕 When is the balance due?

💕 What is the cancellation policy?

💕 Other questions/notes:

Store II	Store III

Notes

Chapter Seven

Details

Beauty

Things to Do

- ☐ Make appointment to try out hairstylist
- ☐ Make appointment to try out makeup artist

Bring to trial run with hairstylist:

- ☐ headpiece
- ☐ photo or sketch of dress to show neckline
- ☐ photos of hairstyles you like
- ☐ Make appointment with hairstylist for wedding day
- ☐ Make appointment with makeup artist for wedding day
- ☐ Make appointment to have manicure (and pedicure, if desired)
- ☐ Make appointments for bridesmaids to have hair, makeup, and/or nails done, if desired
- ☐ Confirm all beauty appointments
- ☐ Obtain lipstick for touch-ups during the wedding
- ☐ Other _____
- ☐ _____

Words to the Wise

✧ Even if you don't usually wear much in the way of cosmetics, it's wise to have your makeup professionally done on your wedding day. For one thing, you'll look and feel beautiful, and for another, a qualified professional will know what to do so that you look your best in the photographs.

✧ Be sure to purchase or get a sample of the same shade of lipstick that your makeup artist uses on you; you'll need it for touch-ups throughout the event.

✧ Wear a button-down shirt when having your hair and makeup done; you don't want to mess up your hair or smudge your makeup by pulling a shirt over your head when it's time to change.

✧ Carry blotting tissues in your purse to keep the inevitable shine (from all the excitement and dancing) off your face. (This shine has a way of showing up in photographs.)

✧ Don't get a fancy new haircut before your wedding; instead, get your hair trimmed about three to four weeks before the big day so that your locks have time to grow in perfectly.

✧ Don't get a facial or any other skin treatments in the two weeks before your wedding. You don't want to risk breaking out or having any other adverse reactions.

✧ Do treat yourself to a manicure and pedicure. The manicure will look just dandy every time someone asks to see your rings, and the pedicure (aside from providing some much needed pampering) will have you ready for the honeymoon.

Questions to Ask: Hair/Makeup

Use this interview for discussions with a hairstylist or a professional who will be doing both your hair and makeup. If you'll be having a different person do your makeup, refer to the interview that begins on page 146 when meeting with a makeup artist.

Salon I

Name: _____

Salon: _____

Address: _____

_____

Phone/Fax: _____

E-mail: _____

❤ Can we schedule a trial run? _____

❤ What is your fee and payment policy? _____

❤ Will you travel? Are there additional fees for parking and travel? _____

❤ Will you stay on hand to help me with my hair, veil, and headpiece (and makeup touch-ups) after the ceremony? At what additional cost, if any? _____

❤ Do you bring your own equipment and hair products (and makeup)? _____

❤ What kind of space and lighting do you need? _____

❤ Will you bring an assistant? _____

❤ Can I meet this assistant? Has this person done styling (and makeup) on his/her own? _____

❤ Will you style my attendants' hair (and do their makeup), or will your assistant? How long will it take, and what is the fee? _____

❤ How long will it take to have my hair (and makeup) done? _____

❤ *If stylist won't be at wedding:* Can you provide me with a hair product (and makeup) for quick fixes (touch-ups)? _____

❤ Other questions/notes: _____

Salon II	Salon III

Questions to Ask: Makeup

Salon I

Name: _____

Salon: _____

Address: _____

_____

_____

Phone/Fax: _____

E-mail: _____

❤ Can we schedule a trial run? _____

❤ What is your fee and payment policy? _____

❤ Will you travel? Are there additional fees for parking and travel? _____

❤ Will you stay on hand for touch-ups after the ceremony and during the reception? At what additional cost? _____

❤ Do you bring your own makeup and brushes? _____

❤ What kind of space and lighting do you need? _____

❤ Will you bring an assistant? _____

❤ Can I meet this assistant? Has this person done makeup on his/her own? _____

❤ Will you do my attendants' makeup, or will your assistant? How long will it take, and what is the fee? _____

❤ How long will it take to have my makeup done? _____

❤ *If makeup artist won't be at wedding:* Can you provide me with makeup for touch-ups during the wedding? _____

❤ Other questions/notes: _____

_____ _____

_____ _____

_____ _____

_____ _____

Salon II	Salon III

Rehearsal Dinner

(While this is traditionally the responsibility of the groom's parents, many brides are involved in planning this event. Use the following according to your needs.)

Things to Do

If groom's parents are planning the event:

- ☐ Discuss rehearsal dinner with groom's parents
- ☐ Give groom's parents the menu for the wedding reception so that the meals are not too similar
- ☐ Compile guest list for rehearsal dinner
- ☐ Give addresses or phone numbers of guests on your list to groom's parents
- ☐ Compose toast (with groom) to thank hosts and guests
- ☐ Other _____
- ☐ _____
- ☐ _____

If bride is involved in planning the event:

- ☐ Reserve location
- ☐ Send signed contract and deposit for location
- ☐ Decide upon menu
- ☐ Make arrangements for any decorations or music
- ☐ Compile guest list (with addresses or phone numbers) for rehearsal dinner
- ☐ Order, purchase, or print out invitations, or call invitees
- ☐ Address invitations
- ☐ Send invitations
- ☐ Compose toast (with groom) to thank hosts and/or guests
- ☐ Give final head count to site manager
- ☐ Confirm all details with site manager
- ☐ Other _____
- ☐ _____
- ☐ _____
- ☐ _____
- ☐ _____

Facts at Your Fingertips: Rehearsal Dinner Basics

✧ **Hosts:** According to traditional practices, the parents of the groom throw this party, but today the celebration can be hosted by both the bride's and groom's parents or by the happy couple themselves.

✧ **Invitees:** Members of the wedding party, immediate family members, and the officiant—as well as the spouses or significant others of all these people—are on the guest list for this event. Often, the hosts choose to invite out-of-town wedding guests as well.

✧ **Style:** Usually a more casual affair than the wedding, the rehearsal dinner can be anything you want, from a sit-down dinner at a restaurant to a laid-back cookout in the backyard.

✧ **Invitations:** These tend to be less formal than those for the wedding. Often, hosts choose the do-it-yourself method rather than having invitations professionally printed. Phone calls are also perfectly appropriate.

✧ **Toasts:** Generally, the hosts of the party toast the bride and groom, as does the best man, but any number of people can stand up to say a few words. It is also gracious for the bride and groom to toast their hosts and thank their guests. Like the overall style of the event, the toasts at the rehearsal dinner tend to be more casual than those given at the wedding, often including amusing stories.

✧ **Gifts:** Many couples take this opportunity to present their gifts to their attendants.

KEEP IN MIND
If the groom's parents are throwing the rehearsal dinner, the immediate family members should be spread out among the tables to better host the guests.

Questions to Ask: Rehearsal Dinner

Site I

Site name:

Contact person:

Address:

Phone/Fax:

E-mail:

❤ How many people can the space accommodate?

❤ Is there a minimum head count required?

❤ Do you offer a buffet or a seated meal?

❤ What are our choices for the menu?

❤ Will you work with us to keep the menu different from that of the wedding?

❤ Can you cater to special dietary needs?

❤ What is the overall fee, and what exactly does that include?

❤ Are gratuities additional?

❤ How many hours are we allotted?

❤ How do overtime charges work?

❤ How do the bar fees work?

❤ What label of alcohol is used?

❤ Can we bring in our own liquor? If so, is there a corkage fee?

Site II	Site III

Site I

❤ How private is the space we'll be using?

❤ Are there any outdoor spaces we can use?

❤ Is there a space for cocktails before the meal?

❤ Will there be a maître d' assigned to our party only?

❤ Will there be wait staff assigned to our party only?

❤ How many guests are seated at each table?

❤ What will the server/guest ratio be?

❤ Do you provide any sort of table decoration, such as candles?

❤ Can we bring in decorations?

❤ Can we visit the space set up for an event?

❤ Is there a coat check? At what additional cost, if any?

❤ Is there valet parking? At what additional cost, if any?

❤ Does the facility have liability insurance?

❤ When do you need the final head count?

❤ How much of a deposit is required?

❤ When is the balance due?

❤ What is your cancellation policy?

❤ Other questions/notes:

Site II	Site III

Rings

Things to Do

- ☐ Have engagement ring insured, if groom has not done so already
- ☐ Select wedding bands
- ☐ Pick up wedding bands from jeweler
- ☐ Bring wedding bands to be engraved
- ☐ Pick up wedding bands from engraver
- ☐ Have engagement ring cleaned (so it's nice and shiny on your wedding day)
- ☐ Give wedding bands to best man
- ☐ Other _____

Questions to Ask: Rings

Store I

Store name: _____

Sales associate: _____

Address: _____

_____

Phone/Fax: _____

E-mail: _____

❤ How long does it take to order rings? _____

❤ Can a ring be resized later, or does the decoration on it prevent this? _____

❤ What are the prices of the bands? _____

_____

❤ Do you engrave? If so, what is the cost? _____

❤ If not, can you recommend a jeweler who engraves? _____

❤ How much of a deposit is required? _____

❤ When is the balance due? _____

❤ What is the cancellation policy? _____

❤ Other questions/notes: _____

_____

_____

KEEP IN MIND

If you're having your wedding bands engraved, you should know that hand engraving makes the deepest cut and, hence, results in a longer-lasting inscription than machine engraving.

Store II	*Store III*

Gifts

Things to Do

- [ ] Register for gifts (this should be done before any pre-wedding parties; it can also be helpful to register before the holidays)
- [ ] Purchase/order/make favors
- [ ] Wrap favors
- [ ] Purchase/order/make gifts for bridal party (groom should do same for groomsmen)
- [ ] Wrap gifts for bridal party (groom should do same for groomsmen's gifts)
- [ ] Purchase gift for groom, if you two are exchanging presents
- [ ] Purchase thank-you gifts for parents
- [ ] Wrap groom's and parents' gifts
- [ ] Plan time to give attendants their gifts (often done at a bridesmaids' luncheon or the rehearsal dinner)
- [ ] Plan time to give groom his gift, if applicable (often done in private the evening before the wedding)
- [ ] Plan time to give parents their presents
- [ ] Bring favors to location the day before the wedding, or assign an attendant the responsibility of getting them there
- [ ] Arrange for table to hold favors
- [ ] Assign someone to set up favors
- [ ] Other _____
- [ ] _____
- [ ] _____

KEEP IN MIND

When deciding where to register, find out if items can be purchased over the phone or online, in case your friends and relatives are unable to go to the store in person. Other questions to ask are: whether gifts can be shipped directly to you; how quickly the registry is updated (you want to avoid getting more than one of the same gift); and what the store's replacement (for gifts that arrive damaged), return, and exchange policies are. Last but not least, find out if the store gives you a discount on registry items that you and your husband purchase after the wedding.

Bride's Emergency Kit

There are a number of items that you should have on hand at the ceremony and reception in case of attire and beauty "emergencies." Organize them into a small bag, and ask one of your attendants or a family member to hold on to it for you or find a place to stash it.

Include:

- ☐ sewing kit
- ☐ tape (for a quick fix to a hem)
- ☐ glue
- ☐ safety pins
- ☐ extra hosiery (in case of runs)
- ☐ clear nail polish (for runs)
- ☐ makeup for touch-ups
- ☐ mirror
- ☐ facial tissues
- ☐ blotting tissues
- ☐ bobby pins
- ☐ comb/hairbrush
- ☐ breath mints
- ☐ headache relief medication
- ☐ stomach relief medication
- ☐ tampons/sanitary napkins

Gratuities

Things to Do

- ☐ Add up gratuities and get crisp bills from bank
- ☐ Place tips in labeled envelopes and seal
- ☐ Assign attendant/family member to hand out tips on wedding day, if host isn't distributing the tips
- ☐ Give tips to assigned person to hand out

Facts at Your Fingertips: Tipping Guide

Use these numbers as a general guide. Not only do local practices vary (you can ask your catering manager or wedding consultant about area standards), but you need to give what works for your budget, what you are comfortable with, and what you feel is deserved. Also, be sure to review your contracts, as the gratuity may already be specified or included in the total fee.

✧ **Wedding consultant:** 15 to 20 percent if booked through an agency; it is not necessary to tip independent consultants, though a personal gift is a thoughtful and appropriate gesture.

✧ **Caterer/banquet manager:** 15 to 20 percent (usually specified in contract and included in total fee).

✧ **Reception site coordinator:** 15 to 20 percent (usually specified in contract and included in total fee).

✧ **Maître d':** 15 to 20 percent (usually specified in contract and included in total fee).

✧ **Wait staff:** 15 to 20 percent total, to be divided among the servers (often noted in contract); give to maître d' to dispense.

✧ **Bartenders:** 5 to 10 percent of bar total.

✧ **Musicians:** $25+ per musician (may be noted in contract).

✧ **Disc jockey:** $25+ if booked through an agency (may be noted in contract); it is not necessary to tip an independent disc jockey.

✧ **Chauffeur(s):** 15 to 20 percent each (may be noted in contract).

✧ **Hairstylist/makeup artist:** 15 to 20 percent if booked through a salon; it is not necessary to tip independent hairstylists or makeup artists.

✧ **Parking attendants:** $1 per car (may be noted in contract); pay ahead of time and request that attendants not accept tips from guests.

✧ **Rest room/coat room attendants:** $1 per guest (may be noted in contract); pay ahead of time and request that attendants not accept tips from guests.

✧ **Delivery people:** $5 to $10 each, depending on time and effort spent.

Notes

Notes

Chapter Eight

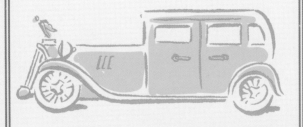

Hotels & Transportation

Hotel Accommodations/Activities

Things to Do

- ☐ Book your hotel room for wedding night
- ☐ Hold block of hotel rooms for out-of-town guests
- ☐ Ask for special code for guests to use when booking rooms in the block
- ☐ Send hotel and transportation information to out-of-town guests; include directions from local airports and cities from which many guests will be arriving by car, as well as information (description, location, phone number) regarding local attractions
- ☐ Put together welcome baskets for guests' rooms
- ☐ Confirm hotel reservation for your wedding night
- ☐ Bring guest baskets to hotel, or assign someone to do so
- ☐ Other _____
- ☐ _____
- ☐ _____
- ☐ _____

KEEP IN MIND

Though certainly not a requirement, welcome baskets are a great way to make your out-of-town guests feel at home when they arrive at the hotel. You could include snacks, a map of the area, a schedule of the weekend's events, and any other items that you think might be useful to your guests—perhaps sunscreen for a wedding at the beach.

Questions to Ask: Wedding Night Reservations

Hotel I

Hotel name: _____

Contact person: _____

Address: _____

_____

_____

Phone/Fax: _____

E-mail: _____

❤ Is there a honeymoon suite? If so, is it available on the date of our wedding? _____

❤ What is the rate for this suite? _____

❤ Is breakfast included in the rate? _____

❤ Are there any special amenities, such as a whirlpool bath, in the honeymoon suite? _____

❤ Can we see the honeymoon suite? _____

❤ What are the rates for other rooms available on our wedding night? _____

❤ Is breakfast included in those rates? _____

❤ What amenities and what size bed do those rooms have? _____

❤ Can we see one of the rooms? _____

❤ Is there room service? _____

❤ *If a summer wedding:* Are the rooms air-conditioned? _____

❤ What is the check-out time? Can we request a late check-out? _____

❤ How much of a deposit, if any, is required? _____

❤ What is the cancellation policy? _____

❤ Other questions/notes: _____

_____   _____

_____   _____

_____   _____

Hotel II	Hotel III

Questions to Ask: Guest Reservations

Hotel I

Hotel name: _____

Contact person: _____

Address: _____

_____

_____

Phone/Fax: _____

E-mail: _____

- Do you offer a special rate for a block of rooms for wedding guests? _____

- What is the regular rate, and what is the discounted rate? _____

- How many rooms can we hold in a block? _____

- How many rooms at the special rate are available on the dates we need them? _____

- Do we incur any charges if not all of the rooms in the block are actually booked by guests? _____

- Is there a minimum number of rooms that must be booked by guests to qualify for the special rate? _____

- Is there a minimum stay? _____

- Is there a date by which guests must reserve rooms in order to receive the special rate? _____

- What amenities are available to guests? _____

- *If a summer wedding:* Are the rooms air-conditioned? _____

- Do you offer shuttle service between the hotel and local airports? If so, is it complimentary? _____

- Is breakfast included in the room rate? _____

- What are the views from the rooms in the discounted block? _____

Hotel II

Hotel III

Hotel I

💌 Can you show us one of the rooms
that would be in the discounted block? _____

💌 Will guests have the choice of
smoking or nonsmoking rooms
in the block?

💌 Will guests have the choice of singles
or doubles in the block?

💌 What are the check-in and check-out
times?

💌 Can we get into rooms prior to our
guests' arrival to leave welcome
baskets, or can we leave them at
the front desk for guests to receive
at check-in?

💌 Are we required to put down a deposit
to hold the block? If so, how much?
Is this deposit refundable?

💌 If we need to cancel the block,
what's your policy?

💌 Are guests required to put down
a deposit? If so, how much?

💌 What is the cancellation policy for
guests?

💌 Other questions/notes:

KEEP IN MIND

A casual brunch on the morning after the wedding provides the opportunity to spend some extra time with out-of-town guests who have come a long way to see you. Such a get-together can be hosted by you and your groom or anyone else who offers.

Hotel II

Hotel III

Notes

Transportation

Things to Do

- [ ] Book/arrange for transportation for bride, groom, wedding party, and immediate family to ceremony and reception
- [ ] Book/arrange for bride and groom's getaway vehicle after reception
- [ ] Book/arrange for transportation for immediate family and wedding party after reception
- [ ] Send signed contract and deposit to transportation service
- [ ] Arrange for someone to drive bride and/or groom's car(s) home after reception, if necessary
- [ ] Arrange for shuttle service to take out-of-town guests from hotel to ceremony and reception sites and back to hotel, if desired
- [ ] Book transportation to airport for honeymoon
- [ ] Give driver(s) all necessary directions, addresses, and contact numbers
- [ ] Confirm all transportation arrangements
- [ ] Fill bride and/or groom's personal car(s) with plenty of gas, if being used on wedding day
- [ ] Other _____
- [ ] _____
- [ ] _____
- [ ] _____
- [ ] _____
- [ ] _____

Words to the Wise

✧ Like all the details of your wedding, the car that you ride in should be perfect in every way. Before hiring the services of any transportation company, inspect the vehicles. Try to see and book the actual cars that you and your group will be using.

✧ A stretch limousine offers plenty of room, but it's not the only option for riding in style; vintage automobiles and horse-drawn carriages are sure to add a touch of romance.

✧ If you're hiring a special vehicle for the day, be sure to let the photographer know; shots of you and your groom stepping out of your "chariot" are not to be missed.

✧ If there are any restrictions regarding decorating your getaway vehicle, be sure to let your wedding party know ahead of time.

✧ Some hosts provide a shuttle service to take guests to and from the hotel and the ceremony and reception sites in order to reduce the possibility of drinking and driving.

Questions to Ask: Transportation

Transportation Service I

Company name:

Contact person:

Address:

Phone/Fax:

E-mail:

💌 What types of cars/limousines/vehicles are available?

💌 How many passengers can the vehicle(s) comfortably accommodate?

💌 Is there a minimum number of hours required?

💌 What is the fee? Is the gratuity included?

💌 What amenities does that rate include?

💌 How many hours does that rate include?

💌 *If an hourly rate:*
When does the clock start—when the driver leaves the base or when passengers are picked up?

Transportation Service II

Transportation Service III

Transportation Service I

❤ How do overtime charges work?

_____

_____

❤ What are the charges for any extra
   amenities (champagne, TV, etc.)
   we might want?

_____

_____

❤ How old are the vehicles?

❤ Can we see the vehicles?

❤ How long has each driver who would
   be providing services for our wedding
   been with your company?

_____

_____

❤ What is the driving record of each
   of these drivers?

_____

_____

_____

❤ Is each of these drivers familiar with
   the area?

❤ How will each driver be dressed?

❤ Do you have liability insurance?

❤ How much of a deposit is required?

❤ When is the balance due?

❤ What is your cancellation policy?

_____

❤ Do you have references?

_____

_____

_____

❤ Other questions/notes:

_____   _____

_____   _____

_____   _____

_____   _____

_____   _____

Transportation Service II   *Transportation Service III*

Notes

Chapter Nine

Honeymoon & Beyond

Honeymoon

Things to Do

- [ ] Get recommendations from friends and family for honeymoon destinations
- [ ] Find travel agent/tour operator specializing in chosen destination, if not making the arrangements yourself
- [ ] Make arrangements to take time off from work for honeymoon
- [ ] Book transportation to destination
- [ ] Book hotel accommodations
- [ ] If renting a car, find out if your automobile insurance covers you on a rental car in the honeymoon location or if you should purchase insurance from the rental company
- [ ] Book car rental/transportation from airport to hotel, if necessary
- [ ] Make sure travel documents (passports, visas, etc.) are current, if traveling out of the country
- [ ] Obtain travel insurance, if desired
- [ ] Purchase guidebooks about destination
- [ ] Purchase foreign language books/tapes, if applicable
- [ ] Make appointments to get any necessary immunizations for foreign travel
- [ ] Book activities
- [ ] Make any necessary dining reservations
- [ ] Purchase any items you need for the trip
- [ ] Pick up tickets/itinerary from travel agent, if they're not being mailed
- [ ] Obtain traveler's checks
- [ ] Change currency, if necessary
- [ ] Pack (include any special gear required for planned activities)
- [ ] Make sure you have extra camera batteries and film
- [ ] Assign someone to keep track of tickets/travel documents so they don't get lost in the wedding mayhem
- [ ] Confirm all reservations
- [ ] Have mail held at post office
- [ ] Call stores where you're registered to hold deliveries
- [ ] Other _____
- [ ] _____
- [ ] _____
- [ ] _____
- [ ] _____
- [ ] _____

Words to the Wise

✧ Even if you're changing your name, book your airline tickets in your maiden name to match your driver's license, passport, or other form of identification necessary for airport checkpoints.

✧ Some airlines and hotels will upgrade honeymoon couples if space permits; inquire when you check in at the airport as well as at your hotel.

✧ Before making hotel reservations, ask for a brochure with photographs to see if you like the look of the place—including the rooms. A travel agency should be able to obtain such a brochure, or the hotel can mail one to you directly. Some hotels also have websites where you can take "virtual tours."

✧ When booking your trip, inquire about travel insurance. Such a policy can protect you from losing money if you need to cancel due to health reasons, family emergencies, or natural disasters; it can also cover theft during the trip. Types and costs vary, but before purchasing a policy, find out if you're already covered by your homeowner's/renter's insurance or your credit card company.

Questions to Ask: Travel Agent

Be sure to go over the information under "Travel Considerations" on page 180 with the travel agent as well.

Travel Agency I

Name of travel agency: _____

Name of agent: _____

Address: _____

_____

Phone/Fax: _____

E-mail: _____

❥ Do you specialize in any specific type of vacation: _____

❥ What do your services include? _____

_____

❥ How long has the agency been in business? _____

Travel Agency II	Travel Agency III

Travel Agency I

❤ Can you make any recommendations
as to where and when we should
travel?

_____
_____
_____
_____
_____

❤ Have you ever visited the destination
we're discussing?

❤ Have you sent many couples to a
particular resort?

_____
_____
_____
_____
_____

❤ Do you have any photos/brochures of
potential hotels (including pictures
of rooms)?

❤ What is the cost of the trip we're
interested in, and what is included?
*(Be sure to get costs for all elements,
such as transportation to destination,
hotel accommodations, car rentals, etc.)*

_____
_____
_____
_____
_____
_____

❤ What type of travel insurance is
offered? What is the additional cost,
if any?

❤ How does payment work?

_____
_____
_____

❤ What is the cancellation policy?

_____

❤ Do you have references?

_____
_____
_____
_____
_____

❤ Other questions/notes:

_____   _____
_____   _____
_____   _____
_____   _____

Travel Agency II	Travel Agency III

Travel Considerations

Option I

Destination

💟 What is the weather like in the destination we're considering at the time we'd be there?

💟 Do we need to be concerned about drinking the water, eating any foods, or any safety issues?

💟 Do we need a passport, a visa, or any other travel documents?

💟 Do we need any immunizations?

💟 What side of the road do people drive on?

Hotel Accommodations

💟 Can we request the following:
　　Room with a view?
　　Room with a patio/terrace?
　　Bed size?
　　Smoking/nonsmoking?
　　Private bath?
💟 What is the room rate?

💟 Are any meals included in the room rate?

💟 What are the amenities in the room (television, phone, alarm clock, radio, air-conditioning, fireplace, minibar/ refrigerator, whirlpool tub, etc.)?

💟 What other amenities does the hotel offer (dining facilities, gym, pool, spa, private beach, etc.)?

Option II

Option III

Option I

♡ Is there room service?

♡ Can we rent sporting equipment (tennis rackets, skis, snorkeling gear, etc.) from the hotel?

♡ Does the hotel offer transportation to and from the airport? If so, is it complimentary?

♡ How much of a deposit, if any, is required for a room reservation?

♡ What is the cancellation policy?

♡ Other questions/notes:

Airplane Reservations

♡ What is the airline fare for the dates and times we want?

♡ What are the terms for changing the dates of reservations after we've booked them?

♡ What is the cancellation policy for the reservations we're considering?

♡ If we're not already members of the frequent flier program, can we join now and receive miles for this trip?

♡ Can we get our seating assignments now?

♡ Can we request special meals for the flight?

♡ Other questions/notes:

Option II

Option III

Option I

Train Reservations

❤ Can we reserve seats?

❤ Are cabins available for longer trips?

❤ Are sleeper seats available for longer trips?

❤ What is the fare for the dates and times we want?

❤ What are the terms for changing the dates of reservations after we've booked them?

❤ What is the cancellation policy?

❤ Is there a dining car?

❤ Can we check luggage?

❤ Is there a limit to the amount of checked or carry-on luggage?

❤ Other questions/notes:

_____

_____

_____

Cruise Reservations

❤ What are the differences between cabin categories—with respect to accommodations and cost?

❤ What is the rate for the cruise we're interested in?

❤ Is the cost of flying to and from port included in the rate?

❤ Are port charges and taxes included?

❤ Is transportation provided between the airport and the ship? If so, is there an additional fee?

❤ Are meals and drinks included in the rate?

Option II	*Option III*

Option I

❤ What are the seating arrangements
for meals?

❤ Can we request an early or late
seating for dinner?

❤ Are a jacket and tie required for meals?

❤ Is there room service?

❤ What amenities are offered on board?

❤ What is the average age of the
passengers?

❤ Do we need a passport for certain
destinations?

❤ What is the payment policy?

❤ What is the cancellation policy?

❤ Other questions/notes:

Rental Cars

❤ What are our options (make, size,
convertible, automatic/standard, air-
conditioning, cassette/CD player, etc.)?

❤ What is the rate?

❤ How does payment work?

❤ What is the cancellation policy?

❤ Other questions/notes:

Option II

Option III

After "I Do"

Things to Do

- [ ] Pick up held mail at post office, upon return from honeymoon
- [ ] Call stores where you've registered to resume gift delivery, upon return from honeymoon
- [ ] Fill out necessary documents to change name legally, if applicable
- [ ] Contact the appropriate agencies/businesses to inform them of name change, if applicable:
    - [ ] Department of Motor Vehicles
    - [ ] passport office
    - [ ] Social Security Administration
    - [ ] insurance agencies
    - [ ] credit card companies
    - [ ] banks/financial institutions
    - [ ] payroll offices
    - [ ] registrar of voters
- [ ] Contact any agencies/businesses that require knowledge of or should know about your change in marital status
- [ ] Send thank-you notes
- [ ] Send change-of-address cards
- [ ] Follow up with photographer regarding proofs
- [ ] Follow up with videographer
- [ ] Other _____
- [ ] _____
- [ ] _____
- [ ] _____

Notes

Notes

Appendix

Gift Registry Guide

	Quantity		Quantity

Formal China

Place settings:

Chargers _____

Dinner plates _____

Salad/dessert plates _____

Bread plates _____

Cups and saucers _____

Rimmed soup bowls _____

Serving pieces:

Large platter _____

Medium platter _____

Covered vegetable
dish _____

Open vegetable dish _____

Gravy boat _____

Creamer _____

Sugar bowl _____

Butter dish _____

Salt and pepper
shakers _____

Everyday Dishes

Place settings:

Dinner plates _____

Salad/dessert plates _____

Soup/cereal bowls _____

Cups and saucers _____

Mugs _____

Serving pieces:

Large platter _____

Medium platter _____

Everyday Dishes (continued)

Covered vegetable
dish _____

Open vegetable dish _____

Salad bowl _____

Salad tongs _____

Creamer _____

Sugar bowl _____

Butter dish _____

Salt and pepper
shakers _____

Crystal/Barware

Red wine glasses _____

White wine glasses _____

Water goblets _____

Highballs _____

Double
old-fashioneds _____

Champagne flutes _____

Decanter _____

Ice bucket
(and tongs) _____

Martini glasses _____

Pilsners _____

Everyday Glassware

Iced tea glasses _____

Juice glasses _____

Pitcher _____

	Sterling Quantity	Stainless Quantity
Flatware		
(sterling and/or stainless)		
Place settings:		
Dinner forks	_____	_____
Salad forks	_____	_____
Dinner knives	_____	_____
Butter knives	_____	_____
Tablespoons	_____	_____
Teaspoons	_____	_____
Soup spoons	_____	_____
Dessert spoons	_____	_____
Iced tea spoons	_____	_____
Serving pieces:		
Serving spoon	_____	_____
Pierced spoon	_____	_____
Serving fork	_____	_____
Cake server	_____	_____
Lasagna server	_____	_____
Ladle	_____	_____

	Quantity
Entertaining	
Cheese board	_____
Cheese knives	_____
Platter for hors	
d'oeuvres	_____
Chip and dip	_____
Cake plate	_____
Coasters	_____
Trivets	_____

	Quantity
Knives	
Steak knives	_____
Bread knife	_____
Chef's knife	_____
Carving knife	_____
Carving fork	_____
Boning knife	_____
Cleaver	_____
Paring knife	_____
Kitchen shears	_____
Sharpening rod	_____
Knife block	_____
Cookware	
1-quart saucepan	_____
2-quart saucepan	_____
3-quart saucepan	_____
Stockpot	_____
2-quart Dutch oven	_____
4-quart Dutch oven	_____
8-quart Dutch oven	_____
8-inch skillet	_____
10-inch skillet	_____
12-inch skillet	_____
3-quart sauté pan	_____
5-quart sauté pan	_____
7-quart sauté pan	_____
Grill pan	_____
Roasting pan	_____
Roasting rack	_____
Griddle	_____
Wok	_____
Double boiler	_____
Steamer basket	_____
Kettle/teapot	_____

	Quantity
Bakeware	
Baking sheet	_____
Loaf pan	_____
Round cake pan	_____
Pie pan	_____
Muffin tin	_____
Glass baking dish	_____
Cooling rack	_____
Kitchen Items	
Cutting board	_____
Colander	_____
Sifter	_____
Mixing bowls	_____
Measuring spoons	_____
Measuring cups	_____
Whisk	_____
Spatulas	_____
Mixing spoons	_____
Baster	_____
Rolling pin	_____
Cheese grater	_____
Garlic press	_____
Garlic roaster	_____
Ice cream scoop	_____
Pasta server	_____
Pizza slicer	_____
Egg slicer	_____
Apple corer	_____
Spoon rest	_____
Spice rack	_____
Sushi set	_____
Chopsticks	_____
Kitchen timer	_____
Cookbooks	_____

	Quantity
Appliances	
Microwave oven	_____
Toaster oven	_____
Food processor	_____
Blender	_____
Hand mixer	_____
Standing mixer	_____
Coffeemaker	_____
Coffee grinder	_____
Cappuccino/espresso maker	_____
Juicer	_____
Waffle iron	_____
Ice cream maker	_____
Electric can opener	_____
Table Linens	
Tablecloth	_____
Silencing cloth	_____
Table runner	_____
Place mats	_____
Dinner napkins	_____
Cocktail napkins	_____
Napkin rings	_____

Bed Linens	Quantity	Giftware	Quantity
Fitted sheets	_____	Vases	_____
Flat sheets	_____	Picture frames	_____
Pillowcases	_____	Candy dishes	_____
Pillows	_____	Candlesticks	_____
Mattress pad	_____	Decorative bowls	_____
Comforter	_____		
Duvet	_____	Luggage	
Duvet cover	_____	Suitcases	_____
Pillow shams	_____	Garment bag	_____
Bed skirt	_____	Duffel bag	_____
Decorative pillows	_____	Carry-on bag	_____
Throw	_____	Luggage cart	_____

Bath Linens/Accessories

Bath sheets	_____
Bath towels	_____
Hand towels	_____
Washcloths	_____
Bath mat	_____
Shower curtain	_____
Soap dish	_____
Toothbrush holder	_____
Tissue holder	_____
Wastebasket	_____

Sample Photography/Videography Shot List

Use the following as a guide and add any detailed variations specific to your situation.

- Bride getting ready
- Groom getting ready

Formal portraits (can be taken before or after ceremony):
- Bride (with and without bouquet)
- Groom
- Bride and groom
- Bride and groom with bride's immediate family
- Bride and groom with groom's immediate family
- Bride and groom with immediate families
- Bride with maid of honor and bridesmaids (with each individually and all together)
- Groom with best man and ushers (with each individually and all together)
- Bride and groom with entire wedding party

Ceremony:
- Venue set up before guests arrive
- Guests arriving/being seated
- Musicians
- Groom at the altar or walking down aisle with parents
- Mother of the bride or bride's parents walking down aisle
- Processional (bridesmaids, flower girl/ring bearer, bride)
- Attendants at altar/seated in pews
- Readers/participants in ceremony
- Reciting of vows
- Exchanging of rings
- Additional ceremony highlights/rituals
- Kiss
- Recessional

Reception:
- Receiving line
- Introduction of bride and groom
- First dance
- Father–daughter dance
- Mother–son dance
- Traditional/religious dance
- Bride dancing with father-in-law
- Groom dancing with mother-in-law
- Parents of bride dancing
- Parents of groom dancing
- Toasts
- Pre-meal prayers
- General dancing
- Table shots
- Centerpiece
- Cake
- Cake-cutting
- Bouquet toss
- Bride and groom with college friends (for alumni magazines)
- Bride and groom leaving reception
- Candids throughout event

Contact Information

Wedding Consultant
Name:
Company:
Address:

Phone/Fax:
E-mail:
Wedding day contact #:

Ceremony Site
Site name:
Contact person:
Address:

Phone/Fax:
E-mail:
Wedding day contact #:

Officiant
Name:
Address:

Phone/Fax:
E-mail:
Wedding day contact #:

Reception Site
Site name: _____
Contact person: _____
Address: _____
_____
_____
_____
Phone/Fax: _____
E-mail: _____
Wedding day contact #: _____

Caterer/Banquet Manager
Name: _____
Company: _____
Address: _____
_____
_____
Phone/Fax: _____
E-mail: _____
Wedding day contact #: _____

Baker/Cake Decorator
Name: _____
Company: _____
Address: _____
_____
_____
Phone/Fax: _____
E-mail: _____
Wedding day contact #: _____

Ceremony Musicians
Name:
Address:

Phone/Fax:
E-mail:
Agency:
Agency representative:
Agent's phone/fax:
Agent's e-mail:
Wedding day contact # for musicians:
Wedding day contact # for agent:

Band/Disc Jockey
Name:
Address:

Phone/Fax:
E-mail:
Agency:
Agency representative:
Agent's phone/fax:
Agent's e-mail:
Wedding day contact # for band/
    disc jockey:
Wedding day contact # for agent:

Florist
Name:
Company:
Address:

Phone/Fax:
E-mail:
Wedding day contact #:

Photographer
Name: _____
Address: _____
_____
_____
_____

Phone/Fax: _____
E-mail: _____
Agency: _____
Agency representative: _____
Agent's phone/fax: _____
Agent's e-mail: _____
Wedding day contact # for photographer: _____
Wedding day contact # for agent: _____

Videographer
Name: _____
Address: _____
_____
_____
_____

Phone/Fax: _____
E-mail: _____
Agency: _____
Agency representative: _____
Agent's phone/fax: _____
Agent's e-mail: _____
Wedding day contact # for videographer: _____
Wedding day contact # for agent: _____

Rental Company
Company name: _____
Contact person: _____
Address: _____
_____
_____
_____

Phone/Fax: _____
E-mail: _____
Wedding day contact #: _____

Bridal Salon
Salon name:
Sales associate:
Address:

Phone/Fax:
E-mail:
Wedding day contact # for seamstress
   (if coming to bustle):

Formalwear Shop
Shop name:
Contact person:
Address:

Phone/Fax:
E-mail:
Wedding day contact #:

Hairstylist
Name:
Salon:
Address:

Phone/Fax:
E-mail:
Wedding day contact #:

Makeup Artist
Name: _____
Salon: _____
Address: _____
_____
_____
_____

Phone/Fax: _____
E-mail: _____
Wedding day contact #: _____

Transportation Service
Company: _____
Contact person: _____
Address: _____
_____
_____
_____

Phone/Fax: _____
E-mail: _____
Wedding day contact #: _____

Hotel #1
Hotel name: _____
Contact person: _____
Address: _____
_____
_____
_____

Phone/Fax: _____
E-mail: _____
Reservation code: _____

Hotel #2:
Hotel name: _____
Contact person: _____
Address: _____
_____
_____
_____

Phone/Fax: _____
E-mail: _____
Reservation code: _____

Bridesmaid #1
Name:
Address:

_____
_____
_____

Phone/Fax:
E-mail:
Wedding day contact #:

_____
_____
_____

Bridesmaid #2
Name:
Address:

_____
_____
_____

Phone/Fax:
E-mail:
Wedding day contact #:

_____
_____
_____

Bridesmaid #3
Name:
Address:

_____
_____
_____

Phone/Fax:
E-mail:
Wedding day contact #:

_____
_____
_____

Bridesmaid #4
Name:
Address:

_____
_____
_____

Phone/Fax:
E-mail:
Wedding day contact #:

_____
_____
_____

Bridesmaid #5
Name: _____
Address: _____
_____
_____
Phone/Fax: _____
E-mail: _____
Wedding day contact #: _____

Usher #1
Name: _____
Address: _____
_____
_____
Phone/Fax: _____
E-mail: _____
Wedding day contact #: _____

Usher #2
Name: _____
Address: _____
_____
_____
Phone/Fax: _____
E-mail: _____
Wedding day contact #: _____

Usher #3
Name: _____
Address: _____
_____
_____
Phone/Fax: _____
E-mail: _____
Wedding day contact #: _____

Usher #4
Name:
Address:

_____

_____

_____

Phone/Fax:
E-mail:
Wedding day contact #:

_____

_____

_____

Usher #5
Name:
Address:

_____

_____

_____

Phone/Fax:
E-mail:
Wedding day contact #:

_____

_____

_____

Reader/Singer #1
Name:
Address:

_____

_____

_____

Phone/Fax:
E-mail:
Wedding day contact #:

_____

_____

_____

Reader/Singer #2
Name:
Address:

_____

_____

_____

Phone/Fax:
E-mail:
Wedding day contact #:

_____

_____

_____

Bride's Parents
Name: _____
Address: _____
                                         _____
                                         _____

Phone/Fax: _____
E-mail: _____
Wedding day contact #:   _____

Name: _____
Address: _____
                                         _____
                                         _____

Phone/Fax: _____
E-mail: _____
Wedding day contact #:   _____

Groom's Parents
Name: _____
Address: _____
                                         _____
                                         _____

Phone/Fax: _____
E-mail: _____
Wedding day contact #:   _____

Name: _____
Address: _____
                                         _____
                                         _____

Phone/Fax: _____
E-mail: _____
Wedding day contact #:   _____

Bridesmaids' Measurements

Bridesmaid #1:
   Bust: _____
   Hips: _____
   Waist: _____
   Height: _____

Bridesmaid #4:
   Bust: _____
   Hips: _____
   Waist: _____
   Height: _____

Bridesmaid #2:
   Bust: _____
   Hips: _____
   Waist: _____
   Height: _____

Bridesmaid #5:
   Bust: _____
   Hips: _____
   Waist: _____
   Height: _____

Bridesmaid #3:
   Bust: _____
   Hips: _____
   Waist: _____
   Height: _____

Things to Bring: Rehearsal/Rehearsal Dinner

It is a good idea to make your own detailed list of "things to bring," complete with all the items specific to your individual situation. Feel free to use the list below as a guide.

☐ Ordered list of paired-off attendants for processional and recessional
☐ List of family members being escorted down aisle
☐ Extra copies of readings/songs for special ceremony participants
☐ Shoes to practice walking down aisle
☐ Ribbon bouquet from shower, if applicable
☐ Gifts for bridesmaids and groomsmen, to give at dinner
☐ Gift for groom (if desired), to be given after dinner
☐ Copy of toast, if giving one

Things to Bring: Wedding Day

It is a good idea to make your own detailed list of "things to bring," complete with all the items specific to your individual situation. Feel free to use the list below as a guide.

- [ ] Wedding gown
- [ ] Veil
- [ ] Headpiece
- [ ] Undergarments
- [ ] Hosiery
- [ ] Shoes
- [ ] Jewelry
- [ ] Purse
- [ ] Bridal emergency kit (see page 157)
- [ ] Steamer, if recommended by bridal salon to take wrinkles out of dress
- [ ] Anything recommended by bridal salon to remove spots from dress
- [ ] Makeup that you want the stylist to use
- [ ] Brush/comb
- [ ] Toothbrush and toothpaste
- [ ] This book (complete with wedding-day contact numbers of service providers)
- [ ] Wine goblet, candleholder, other ceremonial objects
- [ ] Guest book
- [ ] Pen for guest book
- [ ] Copy of vows, if you wish to review before wedding
- [ ] Extra copies of shot list and schedule for photographer and/or videographer
- [ ] Extra copy of schedule of events and announcements for band/disc jockey
- [ ] Extra copy of playlist for band/disc jockey
- [ ] Any CDs still needed by disc jockey
- [ ] Copy of toast, if giving one
- [ ] Copy of gratuity list
- [ ] Gratuities (in sealed, labeled envelopes)
- [ ] Payments for service providers
- [ ] Camera (with extra film and batteries)
- [ ] Rings, if not already with best man
- [ ] Going-away outfit
- [ ] Packed suitcase for wedding night
- [ ] Honeymoon tickets, information, and packed suitcase, if necessary

Index